THE BAD IDEA CATALOG

*10 to 100% Off Everything You'll
NEVER Want and NEVER Need!*

Chris Bittler and Dave Markov

**Andrews McMeel
Publishing**

Kansas City

03 04 05 06 07 MLT 10 9 8 7 6 5 4 3 2 1

Library of Congress Cataloging-in-Publication Data
Bittler, Chris.
  The bad idea catalog : 10 to 100% off everything you'll never want and never need! / Chris Bittler and Dave Markov.
     p. cm.
  ISBN 0-7407-3819-4
  1. American wit and humor. I. Markov, Dave. II. Title.

PN6165.B58 2003
818'.602—dc21   2003043692

This book is a fictional parody for humorous purposes only. All products—except where specifically stated otherwise—are not available for purchase.

ATTENTION: SCHOOLS AND BUSINESSES

To my dad, who lived funny.

—CB

To Wilson Kildare, for the postcards.

—DM

Acknowledgments

Thanks to: Bob and Lori for putting
faith ahead of reason, Bob G. for some of
the good bad ideas incorporated herein,
Nikki for inspiring a few products
and driving me to the airport,
and John D. for the encouragement
and for laughing first and loudest.

A MESSAGE FROM THE PRESIDENT

We at Bad Idea Catalog are justifiably proud of our latest edition of *The Bad Idea Catalog*. Although it's not likely, we hope you find many useful products within these pages. For those who do order products, we think you'll be impressed with our simple return policy.* Remember: Order now or you may think better of it later. Hope your check clears!

Chris Bittler

*NO RETURNS

THE MAKING OF *THE BAD IDEA CATALOG*

The Bad Idea Catalog was founded on a simple premise, a premise with which any unemployed Hollywood screenwriter will concur—consumer research is ruining everything. Too much time and money are wasted on focus groups, market research, and determining whether or not a potential customer base exists prior to selling a product. Sadly, these practices increase the price of the products while benefiting only the manufacturer and retailer. We at Bad Idea Catalog, on the other hand, totally ignore questions of whether anyone will buy the product, thereby passing the savings on to you.

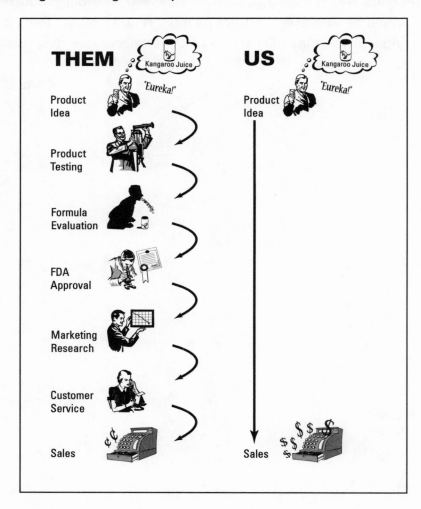

PRODUCT TESTING

Most manufacturers spend vast amounts of money testing potential products for safety, reliability, and just plain does-it-workedness. We skip these luxuries and pass the savings on to you.

BEEFED-UP LEGAL DEPARTMENT

In a litigious world, no matter how thoroughly we educate our customers regarding the potential inconveniences of our products, there will be some who take legal action against us. Conventional wisdom dictates we limit this through product safety testing and settling any civil actions quietly. *The Bad Idea Catalog,* however, takes a different tack. By hiring a massive legal staff and fighting every complaint tooth and nail we come out ahead in the long run—and pass the savings on to you.

Nose Hair Mini-Vacuum

You probably thought using the nose hair trimmer was enough—but what about the unsightly clippings it leaves behind? Oh sure, they're just microns in length, you say. No one notices them.

   Sure, those coworkers in the break room aren't laughing at you and those little nose hairs all over your face. And there's probably some other reason that girl in Purchasing won't go out with you. You could buy this little gizmo just to be on the safe side, but—oh, forget about it. We're sure your life is just fine without it.

Delivered in plain brown wrapper

| 971-005A | Nose Hair Mini-Vacuum | 89.99 |
| 971-005B | AC Adapter | 20.00 |

Inbred Kittens

Unlike any puss you've ever seen! These tensed-up kittens jump, yelp, and run at the slightest provocation. You never know what they'll do next. Hours of fun. Keep away from infants, the elderly, and the feeble. After use, please dispose of in a responsible manner.

| 971-004 | 1.00 or 8.00/dzn. |

Really, REALLY Sharp Scissors

(Not shown)

| 971-035 | 3.90 |

Show Bibles

Authentic, leather-bound King James Bibles are the perfect outward expression of an inner faith. And since it's just for show anyway, it won't matter that the pages are stuck together due to a binding mishap.

971-002A	**Show Bible**	**5.00**
971-002B	**Unopenable Shakespeare**	**5.00**

Meteorite Bolo

Your science teacher friends with their sliced quartz or scorpion-in-acrylic bolos will be forced to admit defeat when you show up at the A. E. Van Vogt Fan Club convention with a whole darn meteor holding your strings together. Specify blue or black string. If subluxation develops, consult chiropractor. 73 lbs.

(Not shown)

971-009   17,775.00

Men's Pant

We've taken off the last *s* for "savings." Another great pickup by Overseas Import Liquidators (OIL). In this case, from an Indian sweatshop busted before the exploited (but highly skilled) workers could sew together both sides of these colorful cotton denim jeans. Mix and match two-pocket left leg and three-pocket right leg for a unique fashion statement. Perfect for irregular-sized customers. OIL logo patch on back pocket. Tailoring services not available. Left leg comes in white, green, olive, and orange; right leg in stonewashed blue, red, and eggplant.

971-001A	**Left Leg**	**3.00 each**
971-001B	**Right Leg**	**3.00 each**

8½ x 11mm Paper

An Office Boy exclusive. Handy as memo paper or for ticker-tape parades. Mostly the parade thing, though. Made in China to American specifications (almost).

971-015A .20/ream

971-015B **3-Hole Punch** .23/ream

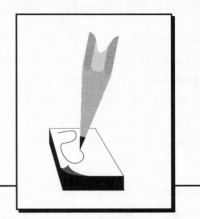

Norman Rockwell Originals

That's right. Original Norman Rockwell pictures. Quality instant photographs of genuine *Saturday Evening Post* covers. Suitable for framing (with very small frames). Each autographed by the photographer.

(Not shown)

971-049 49.95

Mister Genius™ Meat Juicer Deluxe

Save 50 percent. "How about a glass of pork? Or a meat smoothie?" You can whip them up pronto with the new Meat Juicer Deluxe. Powerful 4-hp motor chews up absolutely everything: sinew and bone, thawed and frozen, organic and metal. Generous three-gallon blending bowl makes juicing a snap. Unplug before cleaning. Not to be used in a threatening manner. 73 lbs.

971-003A **Was** ~~229.90~~ **Now 114.90**

971-003B **Lawn Mower Blade Attachment 24.90**

SAVE 50%

Your Face on the *Mona Lisa*

Did you know that the famous da Vinci painting is actually a subtle self-portrait? You might say it was history's first "morph." Now, through the magic of computer graphics, you can be transformed into a member of the opposite sex (or if you're a woman, transformed into a good-looking member of the same sex). A classic twist on the boring old family portrait. Just mail in a photograph with your payment. Three weeks later, you'll receive a genuine lithograph with classy gold-tone wooden frame.

971-007A **Mona "Mia" Lisa (single portrait)** 39.99
971-007B **Mona "Familia" Lisa (family portrait)** 79.99

Flesh-Tone Socks

Perfect for summer, when sandals, thongs, and espadrilles are a fashion necessity. No one will know you're not barefoot until they look close and see you have no toes. Not recommended for people of color.

971-012   9.90 (pkg. of 3)

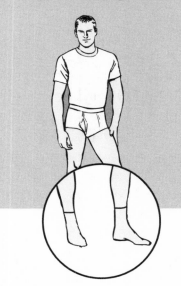

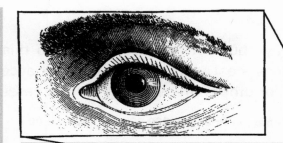

Eye Self-Examination Kit

Explore the mysteries of the human eye with these high-quality Swiss binoculars. Due to a rare manufacturing error, these precision instruments show not a distant object, but a greatly amplified picture of your own peepers. Check for burst capillaries, cataracts, and other conditions before they become a problem. Score another one for Overseas Import Liquidators.

971-008   12.95

Shoe Socks

When you're too lazy to get dressed up. Thick polyester/cotton ankle-length socks sport a realistic faux-shoe print all around. No one will ever notice, and if they do, are they really going to say anything? Blood-resistant treatment for those unavoidable "broken glass" mishaps.

(Not shown)

971-013A	White Cross-Trainer	8.45
971-013B	Brown Wingtip	8.45
971-013C	Black Pump	7.45

Dog Anchor

Your dog will stray—but not too far—chained to this genuine battleship anchor. Half-ton of stainless steel with delicate nautical accenting. Not to be used with canoe, bass boat, or other non-seagoing marine vessel.

971-018   **Original Pentagon Price** ~~250,000.00~~   **Now 4.00**

ALMOST FREE!

6

Wind-Powered Laptop

The ultimate in earth-friendly commuting. 120Mhz Pentium computer goes wherever you and your mountain bike go. Just clip it on the handlebars, deploy the windmill power generator, and you'll be saving time, saving the earth, and getting an aerobic workout all at once.

971-023A	Laptop	999.00
971-023B	Inkjet Backpack Printer	499.00

7

Thoroughbred Bone Sliver Good Luck Charm

Genuine pieces of hoof, skull, or fetlock from some of the greatest horses in racing history: Riva Ridge, Citation, Secretariat, and more. Ideal for the gambling addict in your family. Delivered from glue factory; allow additional time. No animals killed for the express purpose of making this product. Whole organs not available. Specify desired thoroughbred.

971-017   12.95

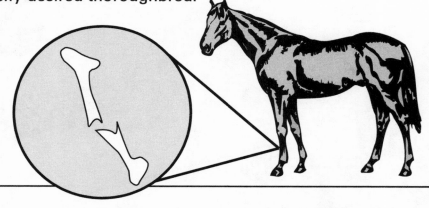

Pet Gravel

When our buyers found a storehouse of imperfect Pet Rocks™ from the 1970s, they wracked their brains to think of a marketing angle. One suggested pulverizing them and packaging them as "Disco Dust." Unfortunately, a cartel in Colombia owns that name. For a while we marketed them as a food additive, but we only got one order (from the UN). Finally, we realized the simplest way is often the best (and always the least work). Ergo—Pet Gravel. Cracked, chipped, and defaced Pet Rocks™ in the original (albeit crushed and torn) packaging, now available to you at the original price. That's quite a savings when you factor in 25 years of inflation. Now if we can just find a warehouse full of decapitated Barbies™ . . .

(Not shown)

971-016 Was 6.95 (1975 dollars) Now 6.95 (current dollars)

Mis-Calculator

A great bargain. Does square roots, amortizations, and compound interest. Just don't multiply 72 by 16 or any of eight other defective calculations (noted in instructions). Vinyl pouch.

971-022   1.50

8

Plutonium Bomb Schematics

A thrilling conversation piece that gives you an air of intelligence, intrigue, and mental instability. Ideal for framing or to leave casually on your credenza. For reasons of national security, one major element is left out of each schematic. If complete plans are received, please return for refund or exchange.

971-027   9.95

Crate o' Mercury

It's a metal! It's a liquid! It's mercury! That's right—512 cubic feet of guaranteed 99 percent pure Hg (as the chemistry nerds call it). And as you'd expect from an element with an atomic weight of 200.59, it has 1,001 uses. Packaged in a handy 8 x 8 x 8' wooden crate with resealable plastic lining. Pickup only; delivery not available. Not to be used as a food additive. Wash hands after use. Lift with legs, not back. 2,300 lbs.

971-006   49.99

The Complete Stallone Collection

Two-volume laser disc collection contains Stallone's complete filmography: *Death Blow, Midnight Cop, Terror in Beverly Hills*—even the comedy classic *The Pink Chiquitas*. All of Frank Stallone's best. (Trivia note: Frank's brother, Sylvester, is a successful actor in his own right.) 2 discs.

971-024   19.90

Roll Your Own!

Toilet paper, that is. Cost-saving kit comes with 200 cardboard rolls and over 6,600 yards of soft, scented two-ply. Gives you something to do when you are on the "throne."

971-038   14.95

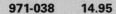

Long-Distance Horseshoe Set

All the fun of horseshoes without the commute. Modified 85mm howitzer lets you "toss a ringer" up to five miles away. Set includes six horseshoes, two posts, two pieces of artillery. Can also be used with lawn darts. Do not overfill. Approx. 4 tons.

971-010   489.90

TP Saver

Another money saver for the porcelain economist. Toilet-paper dispenser has LED display and allows you to both track and ration the number of squares used by each family member. Allows up to 20 personal access codes. An ideal gift for the anal retentive.

971-043   29.90

10

Faces of Minor Injury

Two-hour video contains actual footage of horrifying slivers, painful paper cuts, unexpected toe stubbings, and dreaded "owies" as they actually occur. Adults only.

971-156   19.99

Bowling Ball Key Chain

(Not shown) Specify initials.

971-225   19.99

New Job Smell

A Bad Idea exclusive. Tired of your job but afraid to leave? Office Boy has the answer—just spritz a little New Job Smell around the cubicle and you'll feel like the wet-behind-the-ears new hire you once were. Once the human resource industry's best-kept secret, New Job Smell is a brain-numbing potpourri of particle board, copy machine toner, and all-purpose cleaner sure to snap you back into the semi-hypnotic state upper management looks for and rewards. Instead of grousing about losing your sick time you'll be smiling vacantly as you're awarded a

worthless certificate for being "Recycler of the Year." Phrases like *teamwork, overtime,* and *competitive salary* will take on a positive meaning. Order yourself or sneak an order through your purchasing department. Not recommended for small business owners. Specify aerosol or roll-on.

971-011   14.95

Weed Feed

Weeds are an important addition to any lawn, providing important nutrients and welcome variety to the drab sameness of lush green grass. Weed Feed is designed to keep your crabgrass, Canadian thistle, and dandelions thriving all summer long. Buy a bag for yourself and two or three for your neighbor. Avoid contact with skin and children.

971-21   4.95

Army Surplus Medications

Authentic medications not used due to military downsizing and base closures and now past their expiration dates— but still possibly effective. All manufactured to the specifications of the Pentagon purchasing department. Vacuum sealed in metal alloy tins to keep out radioactive fallout.

971-019A	**Aspirin (5,000/tin)**	**1.00**
971-019B	**Placebo Tablets (5,000/tin)**	**4.00**
971-019C	**Saltpeter (1,000/tin)**	**2.00**
971-019D	**Cyanide (1/pkg.)**	**1.00**
971-019E	**Lysergic Acid Diethylamide (10/blotter)**	**300.00**

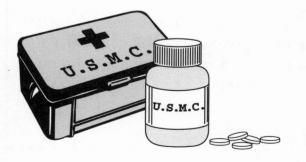

Mister Genius™ Nondrying Paint

Sometimes you just can't tell if a color will work until it's actually on the wall. This product is the answer. Just paint it on, see how it looks, then wipe it off with old newspapers or whatever else is handy. Brushes and rollers clean up with ease. Specify color. 1 gallon.

971-020   14.95

Clothes Compactor

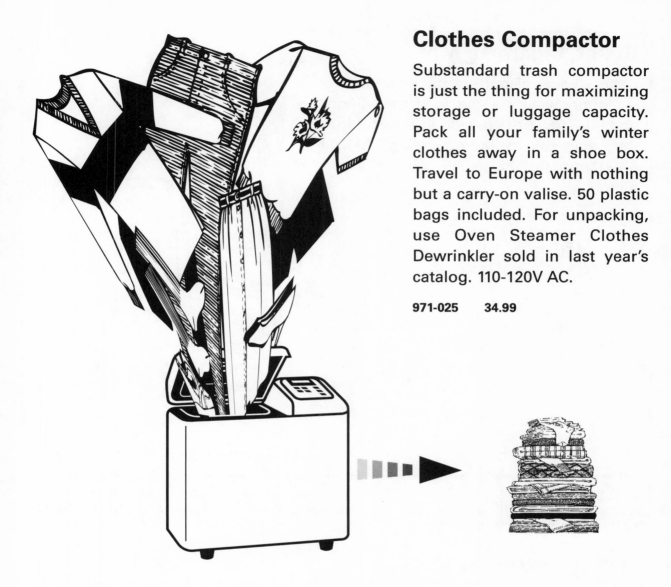

Substandard trash compactor is just the thing for maximizing storage or luggage capacity. Pack all your family's winter clothes away in a shoe box. Travel to Europe with nothing but a carry-on valise. 50 plastic bags included. For unpacking, use Oven Steamer Clothes Dewrinkler sold in last year's catalog. 110-120V AC.

971-025   34.99

10-Second Cassette Tapes

Handy blank chromium oxide cassettes have 1,001 uses. Tape reminders for coworkers and family members. Record your own station IDs. Use them as building blocks.

971-014   .10

Bullet/Cigarette Maker

Choose your poison. Just put your tobacco (or gunpowder) in the loading cylinder and pull down the handle to insert it into the paper roll (or ammo casing). Makes 80–110mm (or .22 to .45 caliber). Clean after use.

971-056   37.99

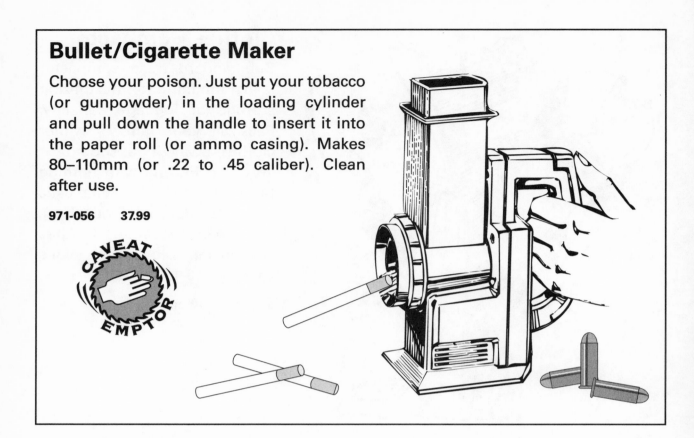

Losing Lottery Numbers

Know what numbers not to pick! An up-to-date compendium of the most unlucky numbers in the country, gleaned from trash cans at gas stations and convenience stores in 43 states. Before you throw more money away on the lottery, throw some at us. Also available on CD-ROM.

(Not shown)

971-028   12.95

Pee Stick

The latest in men's personal hygiene. Eleven-inch plastic ruler (the manufacturer accidentally skipped the "9") directs flow while keeping hands germ-free.

971-33   1.00

Poached Animal Skins

Poaching is a regrettable and reprehensible act—but if the deed is done, why let the merchandise go to waste? Beautiful pelts, quality furs, illegal necklaces—all confiscated by Kenyan Park Rangers who pass on these unfortunate bargains to you. Items and prices vary according to black market rates. Call our 800 number for current information. Please, no inquiries from "Ed Gein" types.

097-026   Seasonal

Obsolete Textbooks

Nowadays the experts don't know anything. Arguments rage on concerning everything from who discovered America to the age of the universe. Why not soothe your mind with one of our genuine obsolete textbooks? Take yourself back to the days when evolution was a fact, Pluto was just a planet, and all the important history was made by rich white non-Canadian males.

971-029A	*European/American History*	2.00
971-029B	*Dick and Jane and Their Big New House*	2.00
971-029C	*Ye Olde Spelling Booke*	2.00
971-029D	*Science Experiments for Young Boys*	2.00

Obsolete Medical Textbooks

One of our best-sellers. Nineteenth-century medical practice is surprisingly similar to that of the modern day. Except for the absence of X rays, painkillers, and sterilization, it's virtually the same. Besides, if you want a leeching done right nowadays, you have to do it yourself. Sure, there's some misinformation here and there in this 488-page tome; but just think how scary today's textbooks will be 100 years from now.

971-030   3.00

Horse Shoes

Another example of the pitfalls of overseas production. These aren't the U-shaped metal thingies, but quality leather dress shoes for the old gray mare. Also fit cows, large dogs, and many zoo animals. Specify brown or black. Sold in fours (2 left, 2 right). 2 pair.

971-039   29.95

Hamburger Helper Helper

This tasty blend of soybean by-product, wood pulp, and unspecified organic matter is an economic substitute for the hamburger you usually add. Very filling. Not more than 10 percent shark chum. 1 lb. bag.

971-041   .30

Stealth Bomber

We're not saying where our buyers got this valuable piece of merchandise. Just place your bid before the Feds start snooping around. Disarmed and unflyable, but has loads of other uses. A handyman special. Fit this fuselage around your high-performance vehicle and you can say good-bye to your radar detector. Agents of hostile foreign governments not eligible for bidding.

971-036   Sealed Bid Only

Vitamin G

No, not really. These mislabeled bottles contain genuine dietary supplements. Anything from vitamin A to zinc. We could figure it out for you, but that would just up the price.

971-042   Bottle of 1,000   1.00

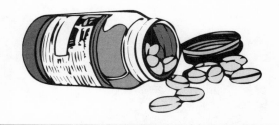

Forever Light

Straight from Chernobyl. These normal-looking light bulbs run virtually forever, with or without electricity. Disregard posted wattages; all bulbs approximately 200W. For outdoor use only.

Avoid prolonged exposure. Do not use near telephone, cable, or electrical power lines. Slightly radiant. Do not look directly at bulb. If dizziness, itching, or tumors persist, consult oncologist.

971-034   2.50

Macrowave Oven

Classic mid-twentieth-century technology gives you more cooking power than you'll ever need in peacetime. Four settings: Alpha, Beta, Gamma, and Defrost. Do not leave living organisms near appliance. Overexposure may cause loss of skin and organs.

971-046   74.90

only
19.95

Tank Turret

Genuine army surplus gun turret from an M-31 tank. Very handy. 60-caliber machine gun not available.

971-032   19.95

Monosyllababble

Tired of getting beat by Scrabble® nerds who put down fake words like "zqght" and "quizicably"? Monosyllababble turns the tables—or should we say tiles? Only one-syllable words may be used. Vowels are worth 10 points, while Z, Q, and X are worth -2. Sure to put your aunt the librarian in her place.

(Not shown)

971-044   17.90

Hum-Dinger

Limited number of these prototypes for the Humvee are now available. All the features of the later model, except with a slightly narrower turning radius. 180"L x 75"H x 30"W. Doors not available.

971-037   24,995.00

HURRY! supplies limited

Golftron 2000

This high-tech gizmo does it all. Gauges wind velocity and direction. Reports temperature and relative humidity. Twelve-wire monitor tracks your blood pressure, brain waves, biorhythms, and blood-alcohol level. Satellite triangulation pinpoints your ball to within two inches. Lightning rod lets you play through the worst of storms. Radar alarm alerts you to other foursomes trying to play through. Recharger for electric carts. Ball and club head cleaner. Uses 40 AAA batteries (not included).

971-59   1.99

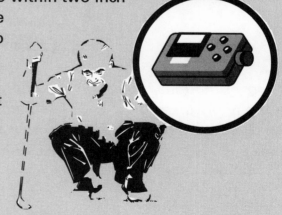

Pay No Taxes
by Albert Bertrand

Take a stand against those fascists at the IRS! Author Albert Bertrand reveals the tax-saving secret of being a Royal Citizen of the United States—one not subject to taxation by the Federal Government. The money you'll save is more than worth the risk of incarceration. Complete with ready-to-copy unofficial forms.

971-031   14.95

"I never thought I could not pay my taxes, but Mr. Bertrand's book makes it easy."
    —Emily Plip,
        Pinckeyhouse, IL

"I simply copied and filled out the Citizenship Renunciation form, mailed it to myself, and changed my address. The IRS hasn't bothered me in over three weeks."
    —Delbert Lequeue,
        Alberta, Canada

"Albert Bertrand has saved me thousands of dollars in taxes over the past 30 months. He is a brilliant accountant and a model prisoner."
    —Harrington S. Moss,
        Warden, Marion
        Correctional Facility

Canceled Utility Bills

Gas, phone, electricity—even cable bills from all fifty states! Compare rates. Use as wallpaper. Great for confetti or performance art. Package of 100.

971-054   1.95

Family Photos

Antique photos of great-great-grandparents, uncles, and other ancestors are the perfect accent for any room. So what if they're not yours? Set of six.

(Not shown)

971-047   19.20

Ironclad Raft

971-053   Was 49.90   Now 4.95

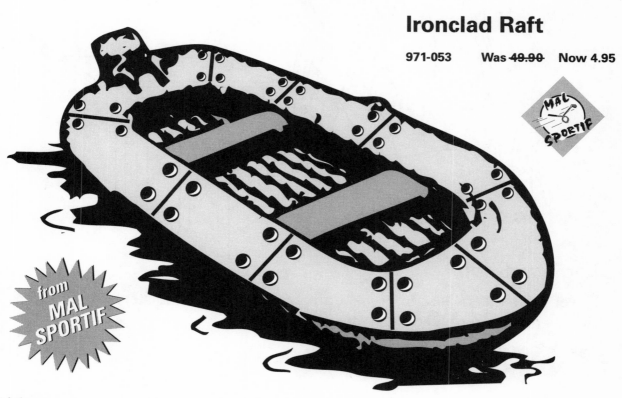

from **MAL SPORTIF**

Mal Sportif Score Buddy

This amazing product takes 18 to 40 strokes off your game. "Pencil eraser" technology makes Score Buddy easy to use. Sharpener included.

971-061   9.95

Excelsior Longjohns

All the insulation of Styrofoam with all the comfort of a beanbag chair. Do not puncture. One size fits many.

(Not shown)

971-051A Men's	**9.95 pair**
971-051B Women's	**14.95 pair**

Legless Chair

Fewer parts means less to break. Comfy, overstuffed upholstery. Treated with Genius-gard™ to prevent dust stains.

971-050   78.50

Mal Sportif Mister Genius™ Mr. Putter Golf Robot

Enjoy the ambience and camaraderie of golf but frustrated with the game itself? Mister Genius™ has the answer. The golf robot stands a mere 27", but it drives, chips, and putts like an aging pro. All you have to do is drive the cart, drink beer, and tell off-color jokes. Special "duffer" setting prevents jealous golf buddies. Wears size 3 golf shoes (not included).

971-060   79.90

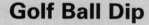

Golf Ball Dip

From Mal Sportif. Heavy-duty acrylic paint system is ideal for rejuvenating those "found" balls. Covers stripes, initials, and other identifying marks permanently and quickly. Not designed for clubs or shoes.

971-058   17.90

Frivolous Lawsuit Handbook.

(Not shown)

971-067   14.95

Static Electricity Toupee

Tired of pesky hairpiece slippage? Mister Genius™ has the solution. Each individual hair of the toupee clings to your head the natural way. No clips or messy adhesives to bother with. Steer clear of balloons and electrical appliances. Specify black, red, or blond.

971-045   34.95

Cat Odometer

Keep track of the wear and tear on your household pet. Who knows, maybe it's tax-deductible.

971-040   4.99

Exposed Film

Its uselessness makes it a bargain. Specify 35mm or 110mm.

971-153A	**24 Pre-exposures**	**.50**
971-153B	**36 Pre-exposures**	**.50**

Junior Electricity Set

Another quality idea from Mister Genius™. Transformers, resistors, bare wire, and more. Just plug it into a 220v power source and give your child an eye-opening scientific experience. Included free: Mister Genius™ Junior Burn Kit.

971-057   39.99

Official Police Officer Kit

You can abuse all the laws real police do when you enlist in the International Police Department. Run red lights. Pull over cute chicks. Get free coffee and pie. Hassle others just because you're in a bad mood. Valid only in U.S. territories of Guam, Puerto Rico, and U.S. Virgin Islands, and the State of Arkansas.

971-062   14.95

Solar-Powered Umbrella

971-052   Was ~~19.95~~   Now 1.95

only
1.95

Mister Genius™ Easy-Find Book Safe

Most safes disguised as books are so convincing you may never find them again. Mister Genius™ has the answer. His book safe has the same lock and unbreakable features as the name brands, plus has BOOK SAFE printed on the spine in orange safety paint. So simple it's a wonder nobody else thought of it first.

971-068A   7.95
971-068B   Easy-Find Wall Safe   17.95

Inspirational Urinal Pads

A Bad Idea exclusive. Did you know the average employee spends over 60 hours in the bathroom per year? What better way to redeem that time than with positive affirmations? Sturdy rubber urinal pads are beautifully illustrated and scented. Choose from the following inspirational messages: "Stress: It's not the pressure, it's how you handle it." "Confidence: If you think you can, you can." "Teamwork: It takes a big man to ask for help." And the perennial favorite: "Aim high." Specify message and color.

971-065A   9.95

971-065B   Women's Restroom Inspirational Graffiti 12.95

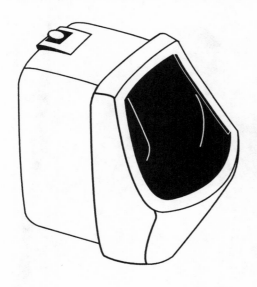

Cake-Scented Urinal Cakes

Edible prior to use.

(Not shown)

971-066   1.09

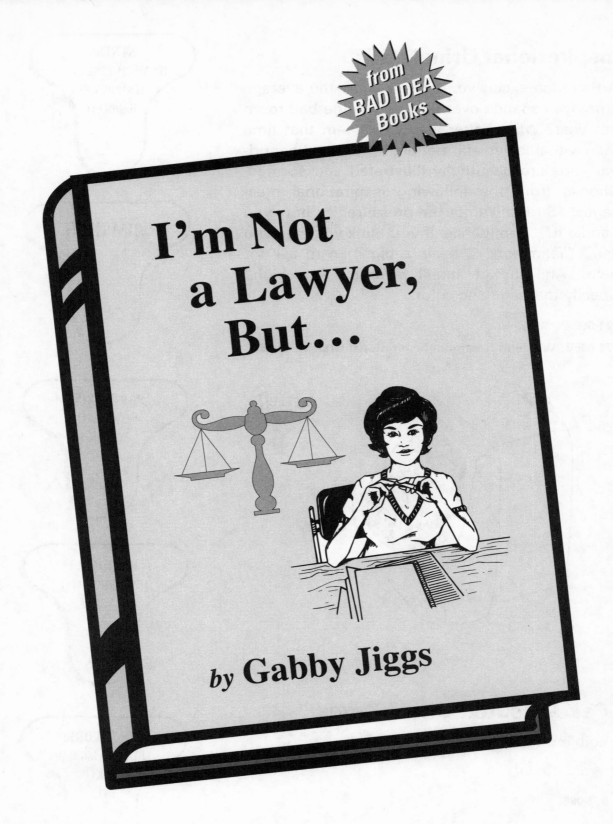

I'm Not
a Lawyer,
But...

by **Gabby Jiggs**

I'm Not a Lawyer, But . . .

by Gabby Jiggs

Tired of getting the runaround from your $150-an-hour shyster? Then Gabby Jiggs's book is for you. It's loaded with off-the-cuff, shoot-from-the-hip legal advice. The kind you'd expect from a temporary legal secretary with over 20 months of experience at 14 different law firms. Gabby tells you how to file a lawsuit, be your own bail bondsman, gain the judge's sympathy, and type and serve your own court documents. With Gabby's system, you don't even need to win the case. If the money you lose is less than what you save in legal fees, you'll come out ahead. As Gabby says, "The courts are a crap shoot anyway."

What the experts are saying about Gabby Jiggs:

"Cheap, straightforward legal advice that six times out of ten is just as legitimate as that of a real attorney."

> —Robert Bork,
> failed Supreme Court candidate

"She sued me—to this day I don't know over what. I paid her a $50 settlement just to get her out of my hair."

> —Mack Demmer,
> friend and neighbor

"Gabby's great! She told me just what I wanted to hear."

> —John Stimpfel,
> Whittier, CA

"She's going to put this law firm out of business."

> —Denise Sklarsky,
> office manager at Gabby's
> last temp assignment

Gabby Jiggs has typed and filed some of the most important briefs in North Dakota history, including *Baker v. Nice Cream, Inc.* and *City of Pierre v. Erskine Janitorial Services.* She has been involved in numerous civil suits as a plaintiff, defendant, or typist, and has filed criminal charges against several friends and neighbors. Gabby has a certificate in word processing with an emphasis on spell-checking. She is currently working on her associate's degree at John Ritter Community College. Gabby does "illegal consulting" on a regular basis; her services may be obtained through Friendly Legal Temporaries, Inc., Pierre, North Dakota.

971-075   24.95

Also available:
I'm Not a Copier Repairman, But . . .
by Gabby Jiggs

(Not shown)

971-076   19.95

29

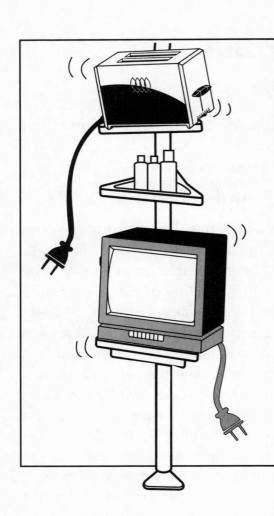

Bath Appliance Shelf

Indulge yourself in the bath. Handy corner shelf holds televisions, radios, space heaters, and other electrical appliances. Built-in four-plug outlet. Economical plastic shelf fastens to tile with adhesive strips. Not recommended for children under two. Keep away from water.

971-072   1.95

Gas-Powered Space Heater

(Not shown)

971-073   19.95

Rhesus Pieces

Chocolate-covered bits of those cute little monkeys used in lab research. Considered a delicacy in some foreign country. 1 lb. bag.

971-069   3.95

Potato Chip Cubes

Approximately ¾" cubes of kettle-fried spud snacks stack neatly on the plate. Perfect for the anal-retentive picnicker. 6 oz. box.

971-081   .99

Ant Jerky

Made from the finest farm-raised black ants. 100 percent rodent-hair free. 1 lb. box.

971-079   8.95

971-080   Ant Licorice (specify
**   black, red, or carpenter)   8.95**

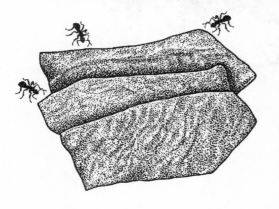

Great Lakes Salmon Steaks

Choice Coho and Schnook from the Gary, Indiana, shoreline are cheaper than the ocean variety and are low enough in PCBs to allow safe consumption of up to 4 oz. per month. Remove cysts (if any) before cooking.

(Not shown)

971-093   1.99 lb.

French Toast Spread

Can't get your kids to eat their veggies? We've got the answer. Specify cinnamon or nutmeg. 64 oz.

971-084   2.95

Doggie Prod

Studies show that choker collars can injure man's best friend. That's why smart pet owners use this low-voltage cattle prod to get Spot up and moving. Uses 20 D batteries (not included). Not recommended for rottweilers, Dobermans, chows, or strays. Not to be used on children or for really funny initiation pranks.

971-078   27.95

Sirloin Turkey

A new take on the old holiday feast. Top sirloin shaped like a roast turkey. Pork "white meat" breast and wings. Order early!

971-085   2.49 lb.

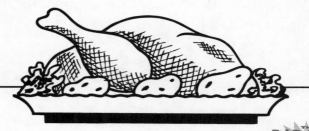

Safety Hammer

Hollow plastic hammer literally won't hurt a fly. Whack anything as hard as you want without effect.

971-086   12.95

Frictionless Shoes

971-089   Was ~~59.90~~ pair   Now 5.95 pair

"Tuba Master" CD Collection

Over eight hours of music from Erik Mehntol, the self-proclaimed "world's greatest tuba-ist." Tracks include "Unchained Melody," "Nadia's Theme," and "Dude Looks Like a Lady." Bonus track: "Ave Maria" by the Three Tuba-ists live at Dodger Stadium. 4 CDs.

971-088   79.95

Leaded Gas Futures

The market for leaded gas is at an all-time low—which is the perfect time to buy! Stock up now and make a killing when the next arch-conservative, states-rights candidate becomes president.

For current quotes and information, call Bad Idea Financial Services.

971-074   Call 1-800-BAD-IDEA

Soda Can Shaker

971-090   Was ~~19.95~~   Now 1.25

Non-Spill Pen

Permanently sealed at both ends. Specify blue or black ink.

971-055   .99

Not-Square Boxes

Factory-reject boxes aren't square on the bottom or sides. Won't hold heavy loads. Don't stack so good either. Good for Christmas decorations, school certificates, and other trash.

971-083   .50

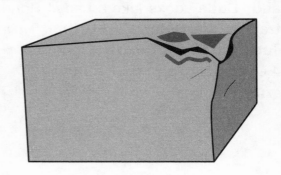

Spike Ladder

Thirty-foot aluminum ladder is designed to stand on its own, thanks to 8" spikes at the base. Tested on lunar surface by crew of *Apollo 16*.

971-095   19.95

Freezer Bern Tartar Sauce Mix

From an old Bern family recipe once thought lost, along with Mr. Bern, on his 1935 voyage to hunt the elusive Breaded Whitefish. Just add mayo, ketchup, relish, balsamic vinegar, and season to taste. Great with Freezer Bern Fish Stick Mash, sold in last year's catalog. 0 oz. pkg.

(Not shown)

971-082   4.95

"the oldest name in frozen foods"

FREEZER BERN

Unwelcome Mat

971-098   Was ~~1.00~~   Now 10.00

GO AWAY

Indestructible Steering Wheel

The last steering wheel you'll ever need. Classic '50s-style chrome wheel won't budge no matter what flies into it.

971-094   14.90

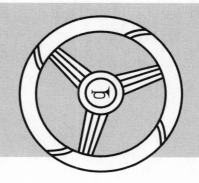

THE BAD IDEA CATALOG

NEW!

Sill Grill

Apartment dwellers, are you going without the simple joys of barbecuing just because you don't have a balcony? Now you can indulge yourself with Sill Grill. This hefty 8" diameter grill hangs right off your windowsill, allowing you to cook up hot dogs, burgers, slabs of ribs (5" maximum length), and other picnic favorites—without leaving your unit! Space-age suction technology (patent pending) and recycled aluminum braces hold Sill Grill in place. Kit includes mesquite chips, spatula, and carbon monoxide monitor. Fire-engine red. Not to be used as a bicycle rack. Do not ignite when pedestrians are present on thoroughfare. Dishwasher safe.

971-112   24.99

Ideal Height Talking Scale

So you weigh 258 pounds—what does that tell you? Our scale gives you useful information—i.e., how tall a person of your weight should be. Quit worrying about losing those 70 pounds and start thinking about how to grow nine inches.

971-064   24.90

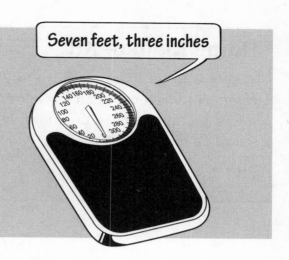

Seven feet, three inches

Home Security TP Dispenser

Provides protection when you're at your most vulnerable. Motion detector monitors window and door. Surveillance cameras check for knife-wielding psychos in shower and towel closet. "Hot Button" brings police right to your bathroom. Secret compartment holds extra roll. Specify white, taupe, pink, light blue, or pastel green.

971-070   27.95

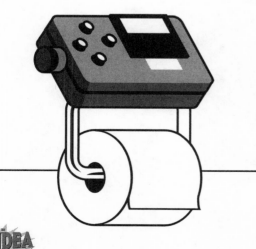

120-Piece Wood Chip Set

How many times have you needed a sliver of wood to fill a hole or prop up a table leg, but couldn't find the right size? This complete wood chip set from Hammerhead Tools is the answer. Sizes range from 1" to 4"; widths from ⅙" to ½". Perfect for both the professional and the weekend handyman. All sizes approximate.

(Not shown)

971-063   29.99

Rain Forest Wood Carvings

Beautiful sculptures from the former jungles of Brazil. All hand-carved by the families of the hardworking loggers who are creating the cattle ranches of tomorrow. One percent of each purchase goes to the Rain Forest Deforestation Project. Every little bit helps. Specify extinct species for sculpture.

(Not shown)

971-071   5.00

Home Manure Kit

Why waste your waste? Turn your basement, crawl space, or airtight guest room into a lucrative home business. No extra supplies required.

971-087   32.90

Stew Table

The fondue of the new millennium. Ultrasmall table forces diners to eat right out of the stewpot or casserole dish—making quality time with the family unavoidable.

971-100A   Stew Table. 15" diam.   19.90

971-100B   Pie Table. 10" diam.   15.90

All-in-One Washtub

Wash dishes, clothes—even yourself—in one timesaving load. Super-large 80-gallon galvanized steel tub provides room for it all, plus as much all-purpose cleaner as you think you need. Wash steak knives and pets separately.

971-091   37.90

Spongy Toilet Seat

Absorbent fabric pulls moisture away from surface—much like a diaper—increasing time between bathroom cleanings. Ideal for bachelors and the incontinent.

971-104   9.90

Prescription Drug Grab Bag

971-108   **49.99**

Mahler's Abridged Symphonies

971-107 (1 CD)

Was ~~29.99~~

Now 28.99

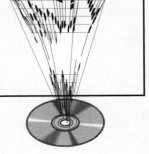

Revolting Coffee Mug

The last coffee cup you'll ever need! Even the most inconsiderate of coworkers will pass on this grotesque 10-ounce mug. Realistic-looking ceramic detailing includes faux doughnut crumbs, lipstick, hair, and mucus. Leave it in the coffee nook with confidence. Do not look at while eating.

(Not shown)

971-215A	Revolting Coffee Mug	16.99
971-215B	Revoltingware Lunch Container	18.99

Coin Goo

You're at an important business meeting or social engagement—when suddenly the coins in your pocket start that annoying jingle. Or worse, they fall out of your pocket. The solution? You could live without coins forever, or control your pocket change with Coin Goo. Just one glop in your pocket creates a single, secure, unified wad of quarters, nickels, and what-have-you. Available in unscented or peppermint goo, to give you that fresh-in-the-pocket feel. Do not ingest via nasal passage. 12 glops per package.

971-113A	Unscented	4.99
971-113B	Peppermint	4.99
971-113C	Jumbo Purse Size. Peppermint only.	6.99

Diplomatic Immunity

Get out of misdemeanors, traffic violations, and most capital offenses as a Monrovian diplomat. This tiny principality in the Pyrenees Mountains is offering diplomatic immunity for a limited time only. Tuxedo/formal gown required.

971-099   199.99

Home Spaying Kit *(Not shown)*

971-105   Was ~~24.99~~   Now 4.99

Acid of the Month Club

Acetic, sulfuric, nitric—a different undiluted acid delivered to your door each month. Great gift idea. Free base neutralizer with initial delivery. Citric acid is edible; most other acids are not. One-year subscription.

971-097   23.90

Picture Cover

Opaque vinyl sheet with elasticized edging protects your favorite painting, photo, or wall hanging from dust and light. Specify color to suit room decor: navy, hunter, peach, persimmon.

971-101   10.00

Menthol T-Shirt

No more messy VapoRub. When your nose is stuffy, the menthol tee will clear it up in a jiff—even when worn under dress shirt and tie. Strong scent lasts through several washings.

971096A	Package of 3	10.00
971-096B	Women's Menthol Camisole	35.00

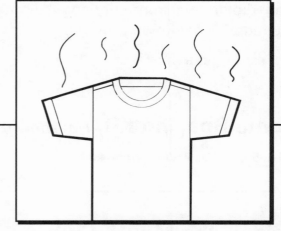

Dud Fireworks

M-80s, zebras, cherry bombs, and more! Great for practical jokes and props. Do not mix with active fireworks. Not legal in Indiana. 2 lb. box.

971-077   1.50

Twin Blade Razor by Lady Genius™

Premium stainless steel blades attached to opposite ends of a wooden handle lets you shave both legs at once. Saves time without sacrificing too much quality or safety. Not to be used as a back scratcher.

971-103   7.99

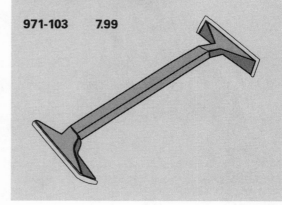

42

Stationary Shaver

Electric razor has its own stand, allowing hands-free shaving. Think of the bathroom time you'll save.

971-117   14.90

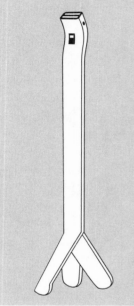

Sieve Spoon

Soup is great—except for that liquid part. Mister Genius™ provides the clever answer with the sieve spoon. Scoops out the noodles and meat, leaving the broth for your uncle with the ulcer. Not recommended for use with cream of celery or sweet potato soups or as a water purifier.

971-114   4.95

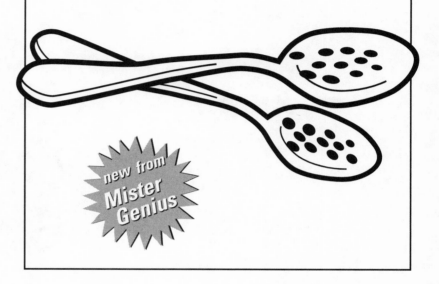

new from **Mister Genius**

Mr. Stain

A toy that spritzes indelible ink. Novelty item only; not to be used as a real toy (or pen).

971-119   17.00

Wally's Pet Attractor

Your dog or cat will never stray again. A spritz or two of Wally's amazing fragrance will keep Fido and Tabby right at your side, where you want them. The all-natural formula, for years known only to sanitation engineers and waste treatment employees, is now available to you as a Bad Idea exclusive. Fairly odorless. Keep away from pets and children. Do not use in wilderness areas.

971-111A	16-oz. Atomizer	9.99
971-111B	20-oz. Refill	6.99

BAD PUP

BAD PUP exclusive

Attitude Watches, Just 10.00!

Now you can own a genuine Rolex, Cartier, or other expensive timepiece for just $10! Imagine the looks on the faces of your coworkers and in-laws as you show off your top-of-the-line, I'm-better-than-you piece of wrist candy. Only you need know you only paid $10—and that the timepiece is damaged beyond repair. Hey, what do you want for ten bucks?

971-123A   10.00

Bad Attitude Watches

Nonfunctioning, with cracked crystal, missing hands, intermittent beeping, or other noticeable defect(s).

971-123B   5.00

Divining Rod and Reel

So you find water with a Y-shaped twig. Then what? With this handy product the answer is—go fish! Complete with hooks, sinkers, bobbers, and 20 feet of 2-lb. test monofilament.

971-118   27.99

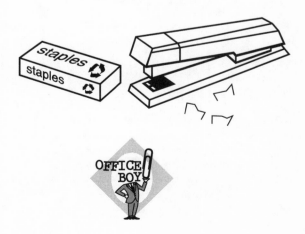

Recycled Staples

Don't ask who had the bad business sense to develop this product, just impress the boss with your cost-cutting savvy. These factory-reconditioned staples work about 50 percent of the time—but they cost one-tenth the price of new ones. Do the math! Box of 2,000.

971-129   .50/box

Harmoniburger

Nothing livens up the boring backyard barbecue like Grandpa wailing away on a chopped sirloin mouth organ. Uniquely shaped baffles make each patty a genuine harmonica. That's right—cool blues hot off the grill! Song/recipe book included. For best musical results, avoid overcooking or topping with cheese. 5 lb. box with 20 quarter-pound patties.

971-200   7.50

Books on Videotape

Read your favorite novel or self-help book from the comfort of your Barca-Lounger. High-quality video recording shows two pages at a time; just press "pause" to read. Go back or leap ahead with "rewind" or "fast forward." Your spouse will never have to read over your shoulder again!

971-115A	*Young Tom Edison*	**9.95**
971-115B	*Canterbury Tales*	**19.95**
971-115C	*Men Are from Mars,*	
	Women are from Venus	**9.95**
971-115D	*Winning Through Intimidation*	**9.95**

Saltepper

A fine blend of premium black pepper and iodized salt. A real time-saver.

971-121   2.90

Bad Breath Arrester

At your wits' end due to that coworker with "buzzard breath"? Stop it now with the Bad Breath Arrester. Proven carrot-and-stick technology puts a strong evergreen-scented air freshener between your nose and the offender's yapper. Also works on outgoing halitosis. From Office Boy.

971-116   3.95

Cork Bat Junior

Give little Billy or Betty that unfair advantage that spells confidence and an improved self-concept. Autographed by Albert Belle.

971-110   23.95

Garlic Lozenges

Reduce cholesterol and mask scent of onions, cigarettes, and alcohol all with one tasty breath mint. Regular or wintergreen.

(Not shown)

971-102   .89

Gluezall

Super-strong iron-acrylic adhesive bonds absolutely anything to absolutely any-thing else. Seals engine blocks instantly. Cements masonry permanently. Fastens artwork indefinitely. Forget about doing it the right way—fix it the Gluezall way. Voids all warranties.

971-122   7.59

Cast-Iron Wingtips

The last pair of dress shoes you'll ever need! In a material as durable as the wingtip styling. Coiled steel laces. One size fits all. If chronic pain, swelling, and/or blistering persist, consult qualified podiatrist. Do not wear during severe storm warnings issued by National Weather Service.

971-126   175.00/pair

Home Medical Kit

Fed up with constant hassles from health insurance companies and HMOs? The Home Medical Kit lets you handle your medical needs "in-house." Eighty-two-piece kit includes everything you're likely to need, from cotton balls to suture thread. Computer Doctor software allows you to diagnose medical conditions with a simple Q&A format. Complete medical dictionary and illustrated instructions are provided on CD format. Free annual updates and subscription to *JCMA* (*Journal of the Canadian Medical Association*). Pharmaceuticals not included. Sterilize all tools prior to use.

(Not shown)

971-139   124.00

Home Eye Surgery Kit

(Not shown)

971-109   Was 107.90   Now 9.90

Very Invisible Ink

A Bad Idea first! Not an old product, but a brand-new one. The latest in invisible writing technology. Long-lasting, nonsmearing, completely invisible ink. Why so cheap? We haven't exactly perfected the chemical to make it visible. But not to worry; it should show itself in about three to five years. Not very practical, but think of the practical joke possibilities!

971-128A   9.95
971-128B   Visible Invisible Ink   8.95

Edible Dirt

No, not really dirt—just a fun way to get your kids to take their vitamins. They may not swallow a pill, but you know they'll lick this fully fortified nauga-soil off their hands. Made from accidentally pulverized famous-maker children's vitamins. May contain recognizable pieces of Flintstones. 2 oz. bottle.

971-120   7.99

Un-Wobbled Table

Sometimes at Bad Idea two seemingly useless products serendipitously fit together like a seven-fingered glove and a Jewish religious symbol (see Menorah Cover in last year's catalog). This time it's a wobbly table and the *Battlestar Galactica Fact Book*. Yep, 126 pages of trivial data about a show you barely remember. Just slip this unreadable trade paperback under the short leg of the elegant Early American–style dining room table and you've got exceptional value. Solid oak/veneer/paper stock.

971-130A   20.00
971-130B   Eight Matching Chairs/Dan Quayle Autobiography   4.95

Dog Training Tapes

Modify your strong-willed pup's behavior via his subconscious. Six instructional messages to choose from, including "I am a good dog," "I will not eat out of the cat litter box," and "I will not lick myself." All messages read by a simulated castrato voice sure to get Rex's attention. All tapes guaranteed against mechanical and material defects. Specify choice:

1—Good Dog
2—No Lick
3—Litter Box No-No
4—Won't Bite Baby
5—No Carpet Whiz
6—No Rug Barf

971-138   5.95 Each

Vermont Wasp Exterminator

Got a nest of pesky mud wasps on your home or property? You could spend your hard-earned cash on a professional, or save money with the Vermont Wasp Exterminator. This traditional system, used in rural New England for over 300 years, is fun, effective, and won't harm the environment. Simply slip on the itchy wool cassock, light the tar-pitch torch, pick up the wooden paddle, and you're ready for some wasp-y fun. No refunds after first use. Not legal in most states, including Vermont.

971-132   17.90

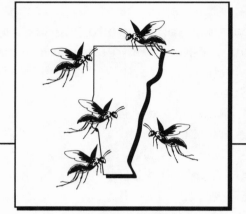

Bowling Ball Shelf

If you're like most Americans, it seems like there's never enough storage space for all your bowling balls. Now Mal Sportif's bowling ball rack lets you take advantage of that extra wall space in the nursery, bathroom, or above the china cabinet. Inexpensive plastic braces save you money in the short run.

971-135   2.45

Hi Karate Wipes

No time to freshen up before that big date? Just rip open a Hi Karate Wipe and smear on the smell. Also handy for disguising gasoline spills at the self-service island. Box of 20. Specify Hi Karate Wipes, Brut Wipes, Old Spice® Wipes, or Wipes Assortment.

971-125   2.00

Skinner Box

Train your children, spouse, or employees with classic behavioral techniques. Sturdy plastic Reward Dispenser can be loaded with 12-ounce cans, candy bars, bananas, or other positive reinforcers. Positive reinforcement can be set to constant, periodic, or variable. Textbook with all pertinent literature included. Negative reinforcement not available.

(Not shown)

971-143A   124.95

Broken Glass Sorter

Mister Genius™ answers another unasked question with this amazing product. A series of perforated trays keeps the large pieces on top and lets smaller pieces fall through—just like a coin sorter! Sorts approx. 5 lbs. of glass per hour.

971-133   24.50

Negative Reinforcer Attachment

Specify electrical shock, verbal abuse, or needle jab.

(Not shown)

971-143B   37.95

Junk Bond Grab Bag

Investment experts agree that this class of high-risk/high-yield certificates are greatly undervalued due to the crash of 2001. Here's your chance to become an investment mogul. Each grab bag contains 100 bonds with a total value (as of December 2000) of anywhere from $15 to $15,000! Take a chance! Note: Each grab bag guaranteed to hold bonds from at least one company not currently in receivership.

(Not shown)

971-127   300.00

Stuffed Grapes

Fine Italian red grapes pitted, stuffed with pimientos, and bottled in virgin olive oil. An acquired taste. 16 oz. bottle.

971-141   12.00

Car Alarm with AM/FM

Scare away would-be car thieves with your favorite radio station or musical artist. Thoughtful "snooze button" function lets neighbors stop the noise with a gentle tap on your hood with a sledgehammer.

971-134   135.90

Baby's First Bowling Ball

Not the full 15-pound variety, of course, but a smaller 10-pound version perfect for your little one. Made of real acrylic to get your youngster used to the feel of the real thing. Includes blower, rosin bag, mini–beer bottle, and stupid-looking shoes. Not to be used on stairs or escalator.

971-140A	**Jet Black**	**14.95**
971-140B	**Blue Show-off Swirl**	**34.95**

Bag o' Screws

All the screws you'll ever need! Wood screws, masonry screws, flathead, round-head, 1", 2½", copper, zinc, and steel—all in various widths and quantities. Several hundred screws in each bag. All swept up off the floor of the famous Hamilton Screw Co. of Hamilton, Hawaii. Each bag approximately 40 lbs. Due to hand sweeping, no two bags are alike. Bad Idea not responsible for any non-screw items in bag.

971-131   1.49

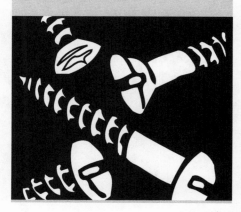

No-Tune Guitar

Famous-maker 6- and 12-string acoustics are factory-tuned. Welded-in-place strings prevent amateurs from meddling with pitch. Avoid changes from temperature or altitude. Return to manufacturer every two years for restringing.

971-144A	**6-string**	**80.00**
971-144B	**12-string**	**160.00**

Gaseous Soup

Did you know that a soup can with a bulging lid may not be contaminated with botulism? Using a simple method, you can test these bloated cans for yourself. If just one in ten is safe to eat, you'll be coming out ahead. Box of 24.

971-148	**2.00**

Your Name in Esperanto

Tell everyone you're a world citizen with a unique T-shirt, sweatshirt, baseball cap, or other appliquéed item of your choice. Your name on the front and a catchy Esperanto phrase on the back. Specify "Mi iris al Londono" or "Kion vi faras?"

(Not shown)

971-137A	**T-shirt**	**19.90**
971-137B	**Sweatshirt**	**24.90**
971-137C	**Baseball Cap**	**12.90**

Aeration Golf Spikes

Patent-leather shoes feature permanent metal spikes a full nine inches long! Provide ample breathing holes for your lawn. Not permitted on most golf courses. Do not leave on waterbed.

971-136   **19.95**

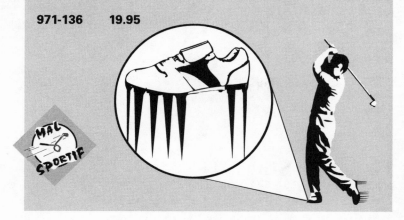

XXX Memo Maker

This saucy software is sure to grab the attention of everyone in the office. Your memos will be talked about for weeks, if not actually read. Photo Gallery application lets you add coworkers' faces to the spicy graphics. 5½" diskette.

971-146   **19.95**

Two-Meter Pencil

The last pencil you'll ever need! Number 2 graphite pencil is over 6 feet long, yet fits most pencil sharpeners. Includes 1- foot eraser.

971-143A		3.95
971-143B	Reinforced Pocket Protector	2.95

Threadbare Electrical Cords

Each has exposed wire somewhere. Find it, tape it up, and you'll be juiced! May have more than one bare spot.

971-149   **1.00**

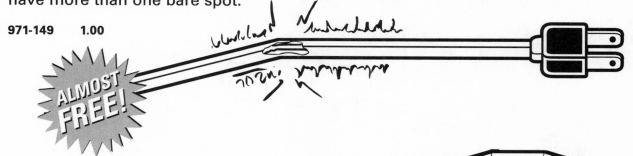

ALMOST FREE!

Novelty T-shirts

Their mistake is your big savings. Cotton/polyester tees featuring various slogans and copyrighted properties we can't mention here. Includes: "I'm with Tupid," "Mickey Muse," "Fathom of the Opera," "Where's the Beet?," and others.

971-155   **4.00**

MAYBE ONBOARD

Human Teeth

Molars, incisors, bicuspids, even wisdom teeth. Collect 'em and trade 'em. Package of 40.

971-150   **5.90**

Dicey Dice

Factory-reject dice add a new element to any boring old board game. Each die could have any combination of dots on each side from one to eight—but none of them has the standard one-through-six configuration. Illegal in New Jersey and Nevada. Set of two.

971-147   **2.00**

Super Jack

Forget the hassle of changing a tire with a jack that barely lifts your car off the ground. Super Jack lifts your car an amazing seven feet in the air! A real time-saver.

971-142   19.95

only 19.95

Celebrity Neckties

Imagine sporting an Italian silk neckpiece once worn by Harrison Ford. Or a power tie formerly belonging to Aaron Spelling. Now you can turn that dream into a probability. These high-quality designer ties are picked up by our sharp-eyed buyers at the Salvation Army resale stores of Beverly Hills, Malibu, Brentwood, and other havens of the rich and famous. As always, we pass the savings—and the residual air of greatness—on to you.

971-152 3.95

Computer Virus CD *(Not shown)*

971-106 Was ~~49.99~~ Now 1.99

Silent Teakettle

Love the soothing taste of herbal tea but get annoyed by the high-pitched whistle of the kettle? Well, put a cork in it! These clever steel teakettles have no noisy whistle, just a screw-on cap that completely seals the container for super-quick heating. Do not leave unattended.

971-158 29.99

Car Baggie

Keep the weather away from your vehicle even when you're away from home. Clever car baggie seals up your car like a peanut butter sandwich. Just drive into the bag, then stomp on the zip close at the top. Do not leave engine running in baggie.

971-157   37.95

GREAT DEAL!

Margarine of the Month

A smorgasbord of lard, from animal-fat oleo to the Norwegian yogurt-based variety. Four 4-ounce sticks from a different "micro-dairy" delivered every 30 days via UPS ground. The perfect gift for your toast-eating friends. One-year subscription.

971-151   19.95

Freezer Bern Fish Stick Balls

Delicious batter-dipped nuggets made from only the freshest fish sticks. From Freezer Bern, the oldest name in frozen foods. 1 lb. (approx. 400 fish stick balls).

971-159   2.00

the oldest name in frozen foods
FREEZER BERN

Ear Canal Brush

Plastic bristles on a flexible metal handle let you reach places Q-Tips can't. Clean all the way up to the eardrum. Do not shove. Box of 100. (If pain or deafness occurs, tell your lawyer you were using Q-Tips—they're the ones with the deep pockets.)

971-165   4.95

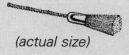

(actual size)

Computer/Television Calibrator

It may look like a simple rubber mallet, but this precision tool is perfectly balanced to have the optimum effect on those disobedient appliances. Not to be used as an attitude adjuster.

971-163   9.90

The Radio Pen

A space saver for the cluttered desk. Prevents hassles from the boss. Specify blue, black, or red; AM/FM or cassette. Runs on two AAA batteries (not included). Headphones included.

971-154   9.99

Two-Sided Garden Tool

It's a litter spear! It's a pitch-fork! It's two sharp tools in one! Do not leave unattended.

971-189   9.90

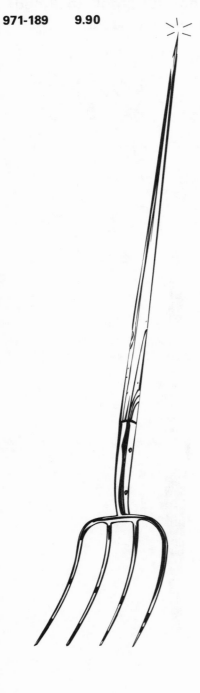

Soap Candy

What manner of demon possessed this famous German confectioner to manufacture several tons of this indigestible (but beauti-fully packaged) product, we can't begin to guess. We're merely passing on the savings to you. We dare you to try to keep a piece down. Great for fraternity hazings!

971-124A   1 lb. Soap Cremes   3.00
971-124B   3.5 lb. Deluxe Sampler   1.00

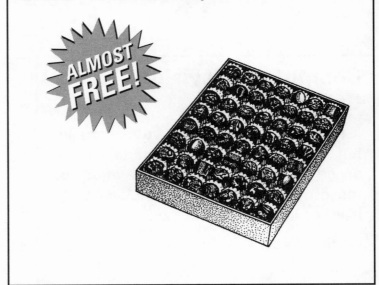

ALMOST FREE!

Mosquito Call

Amaze your friends with your Tarzan-like ability to summon hundreds of friendly little bloodsuckers. Great fun at picnics.

971-166   6.50

THE BAD IDEA CATALOG

Lighter-Than-Air Hats

Never get hat hair again! Tiny pockets of helium keep these quality chapeaus from putting undue weight on your head. Choose from Alpine, Cabbie Tam, and Babushka.

971-161   10.95

Lava-in-a-Box

The ultimate gag. Pour some on your boss's desk and watch the fun as this white-hot magma burns right through to the bedrock! Delivered UPS; use immediately. Price and availability vary depending on worldwide active volcano market.

971-219   Seasonal

Satellite Access

A French communications satellite in a deteriorating orbit is a boon for would-be broadcasters. Erratic beam pattern lets you broadcast to a different nation every night. Say hello to an international friend. Sell your product worldwide. Foment rebellion. Broadcast facilities not included. Offer good until satellite splashdown in or about August 2006.

971-167   79.95

Sun Glasses

No, not sunglasses, but sun glasses. Special ultrapolarized polycarbonate is so effective you can look directly at the sun. Specify frame color. Note: Do not look directly at sun.

971-172   13.99

Vice Presidential Trading Cards

"I'll trade you two Chester A. Arthurs for your Walter Mondale." That will be the happy cry you'll hear once you get your child started on this fascinating hobby. All cards are full color. Career stats and uninteresting anecdotes on back. Package of 10. Sharp sliver of gum included.

971-175   1.95

Tomato Squeezer

No tomato is a match for this pneumatic kitchen appliance. Dishwasher-safe plastic vise holds the fruit in place while powerful cast-iron blocks squish it to a messy pulp. Multiple settings for beefsteak, hothouse, Roma, and cherry varieties. Squeezing of golf balls voids warranty.

971-169   29.95

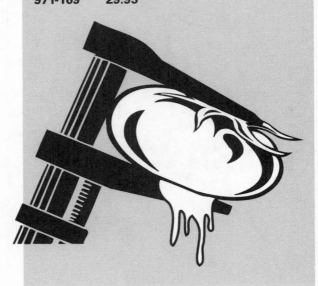

Learn to Draw Good

by Max St. DuPrix

Max St. DuPrix, noted sketch artist and waterfront caricaturist, reveals his secrets for fast and adequate drawing in his fascinating new book. With over twenty years of experience as an amateur courtroom artist in the Quad Cities area, St. DuPrix knows the ins and outs of drawing quickly and accurately without sweating details like shading and perspective. In this 30-page, generously illustrated tome, the author reveals his patented "Drawing Good from the Left Side of the Right Hand" method, a system that is both easy to learn and leaves one hand free for holding beverages. *Learn to Draw Good* is more than a how-to book—it's a money saver as well. It provides names of government agencies that provide free pencils and sharpeners, and even offers a $5 coupon good toward Mr. St. DuPrix's Drawing Good class at the Learning Crawlspace in East Moline, Illinois.

971-188   19.99

from BAD IDEA Books

Freezer Bern Ice Cube Singles

Individually wrapped cubes provide a sanitary alternative to the "communal" (i.e., germ-infested) ice bag or tray. And by using only the cubes you need, you save pennies over the course of a year. Box of 30.

971-309   5.99

Fake Rubber Dog Poop

"Yeeuh!" That's what the office jokester will say when he reaches for this clever novelty item sitting innocently on your desk. Fashioned to look exactly like rubber doggie doo, it's actually the real McCoy. Now *that's* comedy!

(Not shown)

971-308   2.90

Antiqued Furniture

Note the *d* on the end of *antique*. This is because U.S. Customs Service regulations define an antique as an object produced at least 100 years before the date of purchase. But we defy you to see the difference between a nineteenth-century "antique" and these "antiqued" pieces sold here. That's because ours were left outside during a three-month drought and subsequent hail-storm in West Texas. "Antiqued," my foot—these pieces are darn near unrecognizable!

971-195   Your Pick   17.00

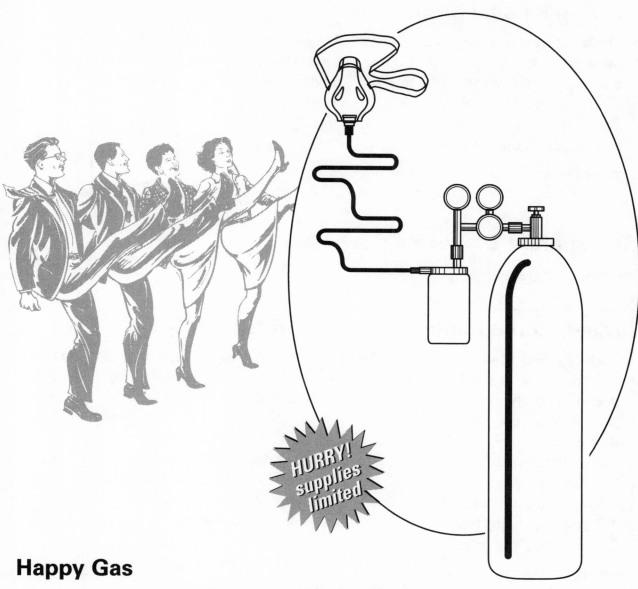

HURRY! supplies limited

Happy Gas

We're not exactly sure what this stuff is, but the buyers are sure having a blast with it. Order a tank before they inhale it all.

971-173   49.95

No-Spill Travel Mug

The last travel mug you'll ever need! Many companies say their mugs won't spill, but ours is the only one that guarantees it. That's because our mug is a hefty 18 pounds. Heavyweight bronze-plated lead provides the maximum in weight with a minimum of mug circumference. Dishwasher safe; radiation-proof. If bronze plating is scratched, please reduce usage.

971-185   2.95

Transparent Diaper Bag *(Not shown)*

971-300   pkg. of 3   6.99

Mis-Colored Markers

Perfectly good felt-tip markers. The only problem is the blue marker is green and the yellow marker is purple and—oh, you get the idea. Box of 12.
1-Blue (green)
2-Yellow (purple)
3-Navy Blue (light blue)
4-Black (midnight blue)
5-Various Colors (red)

971-168   1.50

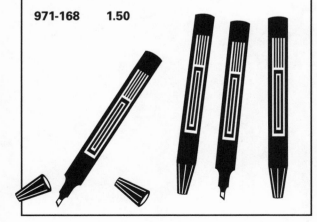

Office Supply Grab Bag

When we terminate an employee here at Bad Idea it's a savings for both us and you. We demand the same amount of work from fewer workers, and you get the contents of the ex-employee's cubicle. Binder clips, rubber bands, doodle paper, corporate knickknacks, old cocoa packets, and much, much more. American currency and prescription drugs remain the property of Bad Idea, Inc.

971-183   4.95

Bear Sneeze Spray

This blend of organic irritants will send a fearsome grizzly into a sneezing fit, stopping it in its tracks and giving you time to escape. Note: Sneezing may enrage bear; run fast.

971-181   3.50

Bad Idea On-line

Paying too much for your current on-line service? Switch to Bad Idea On-line. Browse features like the Weekly Reader News Wire, Winchell's Donuts Product List, Maria Shriver Movie Reviews, Grumman's Encyclopedia of Soil, and not much more. No-busy-signal guarantee. Access phone number via U.S. Virgin Islands. One-year subscription.

971-180   3.00

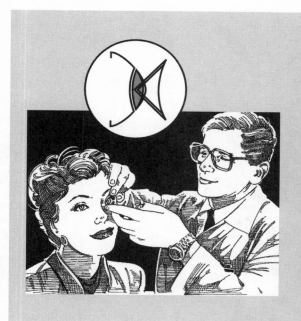

Universal Contact Lenses

Nearsighted, schmear-sighted. For most people, the main problem is everything looks too small and fuzzy. These magnifying lenses are guaranteed to improve your vision without the added expense of fittings and prescriptions. Just slip them in and go about your business. Not recommended for truck drivers or surgeons. For farsightedness, flip lenses inside out.

971-164A	24.00	
971-164B	Self-tinting Solution	2.00

The Seven Habits of Successful Serial Killers
by Pradeep Kepmash

"Serial killers are not born, they are made," Kepmash says in his insightful self-help book. "And the same traits that made them successful in the field of homicide can be applied to the fields of management, acting, and, of course, politics." Chapters include: "Displacing Anger Productively," "Abusive Parents—Inside Track to Success," and "Choosing the Murder Weapon for You." Foreword by Richard Ramirez.

971-176   7.95

from BAD IDEA Books

Super Sticky Notes

Memos they won't forget—because they can't be removed. Do not use on exposed skin. Package of 3.

971-162   4.95

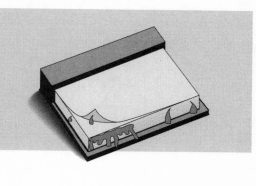

Bat Whistle

Contrary to popular opinion, bats do not drink blood. They eat insects—which makes them the perfect guest at your next outdoor soiree. A periodic toot of the whistle brings a friendly horde of these flying mammals into your yard, where they will feast on those pesky mosquitoes, June bugs, and flying ants. Hair covering suggested. Not to be used with Bird Zapper sold on page 82.

971-192   7.98

Mini-Crematorium

Tired of taking out the trash? Incinerate it quickly and cleanly with your own 3,000-degree (Celsius) crematorium. Includes residue stick, oven mitts, and cigarette-lighter power adapter.

971-092   299.99

Doggie Door

Freedom for the pooch, style and security for you. Fully functional mini-door is a perfect match of the attached front door, right down to the brass doorknob and dead bolt. Leave your home for the day or the week secure in the knowledge that your dog can get out but thieves can't get in. 20 lbs., 3 oz.

971-194   24.99

Cockroach Farm

Did you know cockroaches are more active and reproduce twice as fast as ants? Yet most people still prefer an ant farm to this nearly identical product. Don't be taken in by the pro-ant lobby—order your roach farm today!

971-178   9.99

Solar Systems

Through a legal agreement with the government of Zambia, Bad Idea can now offer deeds for the solar system of your choice. Just think—a medium-sized star and any number of planets at your disposal. Develop them as you see fit. Be the Donald Trump of the Crab Nebula. Plus, Zambia will print a series of stamps in honor of each purchaser. Systems in Milky Way Galaxy excluded. Transportation not included. Water and other utilities not available in most instances.

971-182   995.00

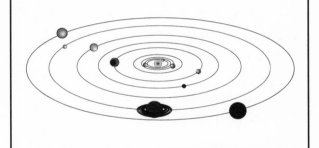

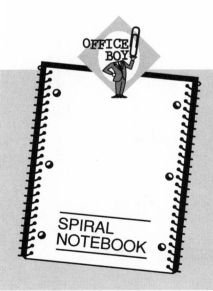

Double-Spiral Notebook

An Office Boy exclusive. Metal spirals down both the left and right sides of these 120-sheet notebooks guarantee cover and paper will remain in perfect condition. Left-handed version also available. Great for physical education majors and chiropractic students.

971-184 1.20

Graduation Tassels

You may not have a degree from Harvard, but there's no law against having a graduation tassel from there (except in the Commonwealth of Massachusetts, that is). Impress your coworkers at the DMV. Specify college, university, or trade school.

971-179   49.99

Threadless Bolts

(Not shown) Bag of 100.

971-303   .99

Roof Skis

All the fun of downhill skiing without the snow or travel. Durable "tank-tread" skis whisk you quickly down from the peak. Before you can say "traction," you'll be climbing back up for more.

971-171   17.95 pair

Rain Gauge Hat

Overstock from a famous outdoors apparel retailer. Wicker safari hat with cylinder on top tells you exactly how much precipitation is pouring down on you as you stand outside in the storm. The ideal science project.

971-177   11.90

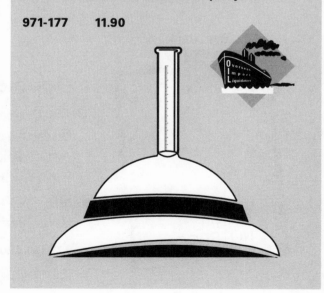

Turtle Nip

Liven up those slow-moving reptiles with just a whiff of Turtle Nip! Your hard-shelled pet will be running, jumping, and snapping like a pup for up to 25 minutes when it plays with this unbreakable, chemical-laced chew toy. May cause cardiac arrest or stroke; but it's a turtle, so what's the diff? Box of 10.

971-191   3.49

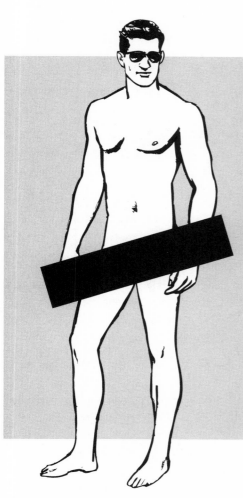

Crepe-Paper Swimsuits

Not for the introverted or the less than well-endowed. In fact, we can't imagine what kind of weirdo would wear these flimsy pieces of beachwear that not only become invisible when wet, but often fall apart. Still, it's a free country and we've got a whole truckload of this stuff. They'd make good gag gifts. Yeah, let's go with that.

971-193A	**Crepe-Paper Swimsuit for Him**	**4.98**
971-193B	**Crepe-Paper Swimsuit for Her**	**9.98**

Unbreakable Toothpick

The last toothpick you'll ever need! Amazing "breathing" polymers allow this formidable dental hygiene tool to maintain its size, shape, and tensile qualities in any environment, from Antarctica to the surface of the sun. Designed by those inscrutable Red Chinese scientists for their long-since-abandoned manned mission to Mars. (Yes, the same people who brought you our popular Asteroid Repellant!) Toothpick is waterproof to 400 meters. Clip-on vinyl case included. Mild radiation emission (24 rads per hour).

971-221   Was ~~79.99~~   Now 119.90

SAVE 75%

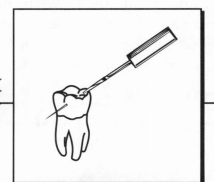

Shorts Shirt

A gross tailoring disaster in former East Germany (where else?) brings us this new fashion trend—shorts you wear as a halter top. A misplaced button fly provides a unique hidden-placket neck. Short sleeves. Traditional jeans styling in garment-washed indigo cotton denim. Belt loops at midriff can be used as "modesty" drawstring close. Order three sizes larger than normal waist.

971-198   12.99 "pair"

Cacophonous Wind Chimes

The loudest wind chimes you'll ever own—guaranteed. Delicately strung ball bearings, tin sheets, broken glass, and whistles create an unforgettable sound that can be heard up to one mile away.

(Not shown)

971-471   19.95 each

Golf Glove Jacket

Impressive leather-like, button-front duster is made from the same high-quality material used to make golf gloves—dog scrotums. Specify size, color, and breed.

(Not shown)

971-170   24.95

The Onion Suit

Expertly tailored two-piece has the same stately texture as onion-skin paper. Do not clean. Do not expose to water. Edible. Double-breasted.

971-220   17.00

Third World Slave Labor

Better, actually. You couldn't feed and house a slave for the eight cents a day you'll be paying each of these workers unwise enough to be born on the poor side of the Pacific Rim. Overseas Import Liquidators (OIL) oversees the manufacturing for a modest percentage and you take the lion's share of the obscene profits. It just shows you that any American can make it big so long as there are poor countries to exploit. Cost breakdown: $29.12/annum (365 days, less Christmas holiday), plus $5.88 OIL commission.

(Not shown)

971-213   Exploited Worker   35.00

Heated Shoes

Never get cold feet again. Just slip on these heated shoes and you'll have toasty feet wherever you go. Electric heating element uses 110–120V AC current. 18-foot cord, car lighter adapter included. UL disapproved.

971-160   17.95 pair

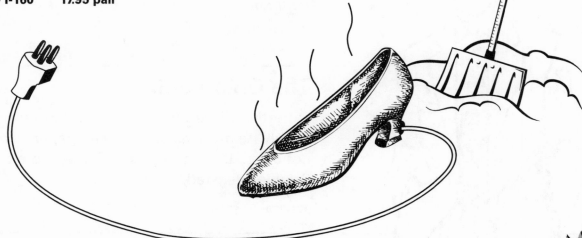

SAVE 90%

Tree Prostheses

Don't chop down that dying oak tree—restore it to its original luster with these realistic limbs. Hand-painted resin and silk leaves. Specify oak, elm, maple, or conifer.

(Not shown)

971-224A	Tree Prosthesis	7.79
971-224B	Faux Stump	9.79

Home Lighting Sensor

Motion-sensitive device saves you hundreds in electricity bills by automatically turning off your lights when no one is home. Frankly, it's a mystery to us why these haven't been selling.

(Not shown)

971-206	Was ~~149.00~~	Now 14.90

THE BAD IDEA CATALOG

Gas-Powered Bike Headlight

Talk about energy conservation! This handy device saves your legs the added work of powering that dorky little generator. Efficient ¾-hp engine runs on "cornahol" and helps scare off pesky bike-chasing mutts as well. For best results, do not mount the engine on handlebars. (73 lbs.)

971-204   49.00

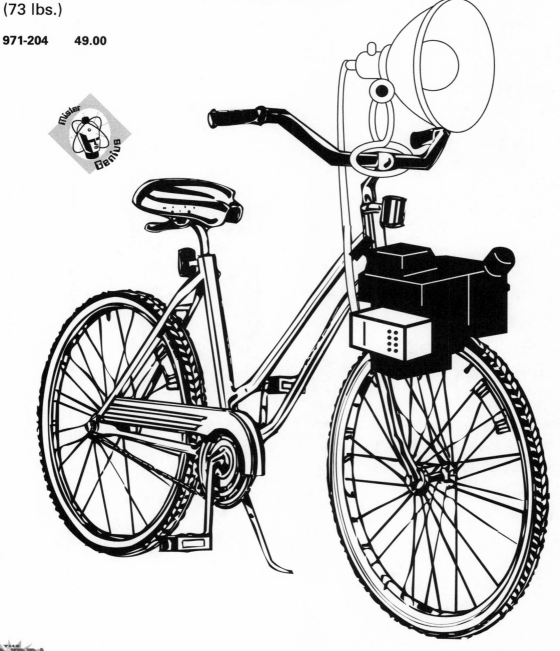

Fishcicles

The same great taste of sushi, only it keeps better 'cause it's frozen solid. Yellowfin tuna, blowfish, squid—even that spiny crustacean thing they crack open while it's still alive. Yum-my! From Freezer Bern. 1 lb. box.

971-187A	Fishcicles	4.98
971-187B	Minnow Bon-Bons	2.98

the oldest name in frozen foods

FREEZER BERN

Factory Refurbished Sandwich Bags

Slight imperfections render these bags air- and water-permeable. A great bargain. Note: may be used as a toy; may not be used as a flotation device. Package of 100.

(Not shown)

971-222   .99

Charismatic Arm Brace

This hospital supply overstock is sure to be a blessing for Pentecostals, Shakers, and other over-exuberant worshipers. When the spirit is willing but the flesh (specifically the tricep) is weak, Charismatic Arm Braces keep the revival going.

971-199   **Suggested Offering of 50.00**

SAVE 50%

THE BAD IDEA CATALOG

Antique Food

Genuine nineteenth-century victuals recently unearthed in Mississippi date back to the Battle of Vicksburg in 1863. Coffee, beans, hardtack, nassau bacon, and more.

(Not shown)

971-048   3.00 each

1,001 Minority Jokes

Positive societal changes have made this literary classic an absolute steal. More fun than a barrel of Swedes! Not intended to demean micks, krauts, wops, hebes, or other minority groups (except Canadians).

(Not shown)

971-174   2.95

Halogen Hat

971-302   8.90

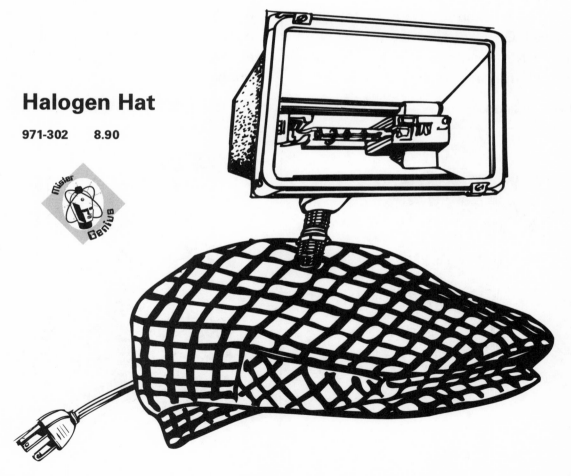

Mexican Jumping Beer

Live but harmless organisms make this quality rice beer come to life. Amaze your friends. Win bar bets. Bring lots of napkins. Note: "Harmless organisms" may cause vomiting. 6 12-oz. bottles.

971-209   6.99

Bird Zapper

Just like the other kind, only bigger. Burns up anything from a sparrow to a seagull in seconds. Perfect for use with Sill Grill sold on page 36. Not legal in Minnesota or Wisconsin during duck hunting season. 2 lb., 1 oz.

971-205   24.99

Beef Remnants

We don't know exactly what parts these are, but they're definitely beef, which is more than you can say about most hot dogs. All guaranteed to have at one time been severed from high-quality cuts of corn-fed cattle. 2 lb. box.

971-210   .99

Mmmm . . . !
Hmmm . . . ?

Aluminum Lung

Don't let your physical challenge keep you from having an active life. Lightweight version of the iron lung goes anywhere you go: the beach, the health club, even the ball game. Avoid direct sunlight. Avoid tipping over in water. Do not puncture. 7 oz.

971-212   99.99

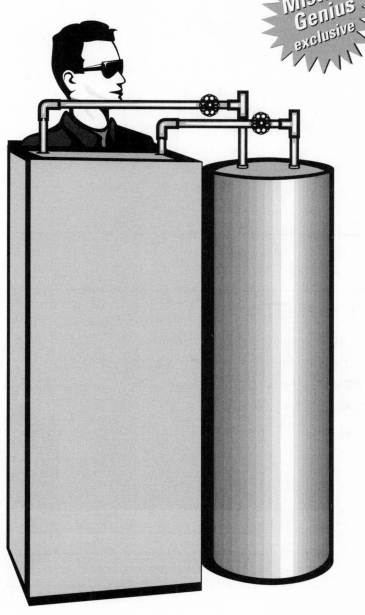

One-Ounce Soda Cans

Freezer Bern ventures into the refrigerator with a variety of tasty soft drinks, all in handy single-ounce cans. They're perfect for those annoying "one-sip-and-go" children and dandified females. 6 pack. Specify Sugar Shack Cola, Limey Citrus, Peat Moss Root Beer, Bitter Pill Dietetic Cola, or Sour Grape.

971-311   2.99

40-Grit Facial Tissue

Throw away those wimpy soft tissues. These optimum-friction sheets make every swipe and blow count. Reusable. 10 per box.

971-310   2.00

Bilious Bill

The doll with the delicate stomach. Poor Bill burps, belches, and passes wind at the most inappropriate times, teaching children a valuable lesson in proper diet and behavior. Tweak his nose and Bill even sneezes realistic "snot." From Don't Touch My Toy. Uses one 9V battery (not included— and good luck finding one). Do not hold upside down.

971-202A	Bilious Bill Action Figure	19.99
971-202B	Bilious Bill Clean-Up Kit	39.99
971-202C	Bilious Bill Commando Set	14.99
971-202D	Incontinent Inga	4.99

Three-Ton Metal Thing

We don't know what it is. We don't know what it can do. If you want it, come and get it. It's blocking the elevators.

(Not shown)

971-216   FREE

Carpet Circles

The flaw is obvious to some, subtle to others. It's the others we're after. 1 foot diameter; box of 25.

(Not shown)

971-217   20.00

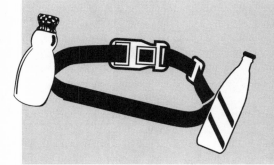

Barbecue Sauce Belt

When you're served Indian or other inedible foods, what do you do? A squirt of tasty barbecue sauce usually does the trick. And nobody has to know you're a rube. Fits waists 30 to 44.

971-218   8.99

THE
BAD IDEA
CATALOG

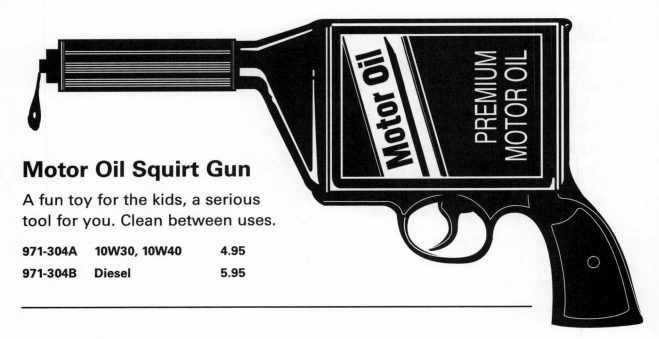

Motor Oil Squirt Gun

A fun toy for the kids, a serious tool for you. Clean between uses.

| 971-304A | 10W30, 10W40 | 4.95 |
| 971-304B | Diesel | 5.95 |

Moon Rocks

Well, that's what the Russian businessmen told us they were. And they are pretty sparkly. So either they're genuine moon rocks or gold nuggets. Either way, they're a bargain at $10 a pound.

| 971-186 | 10.00 |

Crappaccino

An admittedly inferior product from Alberta, Canada, where they wouldn't know a good cup of joe if you poured it down their dungarees. Still, caffeine is caffeine. Just dump a lot of nondairy creamer in it and you'll never know the difference. Whole and partial bean. Substantial discount available to prisons, hospitals, and other institutional accounts. 5 lb. bag.

| 971-190 | 1.13 |

"the oldest name in frozen foods" **FREEZER BERN**

BAD IDEA CATALOG

Fiberglass Shirt

The last shirt you'll ever need! These finely detailed dress shirts are used in wax museums around the world. Best when used with vinyl underwear sold in the 1999 catalog. Some itching and binding may occur. Specify neck size.

971-214   17.99

Grub Pops

Forget it. There's no way I can justify this product. I quit! Keep frozen. Box of 48.

971-211   1.49

the oldest name in frozen foods
FREEZER BERN

The Caffeine Patch

Get that java monkey off your back safely and gradually. Or just give yourself a quick pick-me-up when you don't have time to stop for a double espresso. Precisely measured dosages can be applied directly to the skin or brewed up in hot water, but not both. Sugar and creamer not included.

971-305A	**Single-Person Kit**	**24.99**
971-305B	**Office Pack**	**104.99**

Portable Deprivation Tank

The perfect stress-beater for the Type A personality. Want the benefits of total sensory deprivation but don't have the time? This self-contained unit goes wherever you go. The hydro-helmet puts your head in a soothing aquatic environment while providing ample oxygen through the handy vulcanized rubber hose. The pressurized suit, meanwhile, administers small bursts of local anesthetic, rendering you virtually senseless. Perfect for plane trips, train rides, and MIS meetings. Not to be used as a flotation device.

971-307   499.99

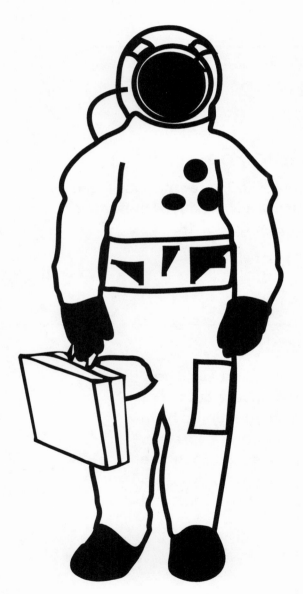

Mini–Power Line

A friend of ours swears that her cousin, a scientist, says there are positive benefits from living near electrical power lines. Such alleged benefits as hair growth, increased libido, and improved TV reception have been reported by this reliable source. If you are already soothed to sleep by the reassuring hum of 12,000 amps running above your head, thank your personal deity. For the rest of you, it's time to pick up this handy desktop replica and find out what all the fuss is about. Involuntary malignancies and/or radio reception may develop. Not legal in most incorporated areas (except in Canada). 2 lbs., 7 oz.

971-203   14.90

Glove Covers

Grossly oversized surgical gloves are ideal for keeping your winter gloves clean and germ-free. Fits over absolutely any size glove. Not intended for use as giant water balloons that work really great with Giant Inner-Tube Slingshot sold in 1997 catalog. One size fits everybody.

971-197 $1.98 pair

Stray Dog Flypaper

Take care of the mongrel that's been soiling your lawn once and for all. Also works on raccoons and Peeping Toms. Use caution when handling; not to be unrolled in high winds. 6 feet x 12 yards.

971-207   24.99/roll

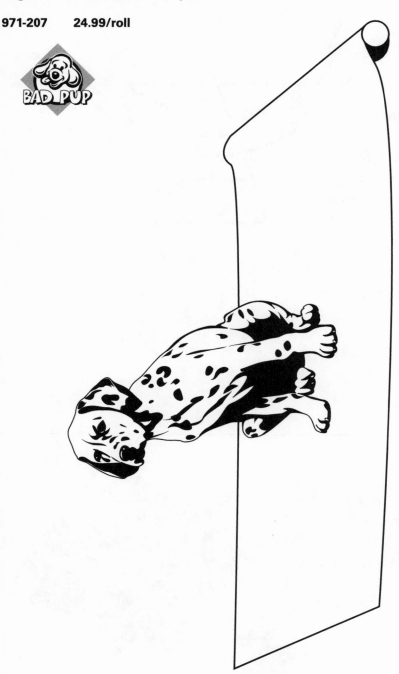

Cookie Laser Printer

Inferior Soviet-bloc technology comes to fruition thanks to Yankee ingenuity (and OIL). A faulty heating element makes this Uzbekistani-built laser printer a hazard in the office but a cream puff in the kitchen. Just put your cookie dough in the paper tray and "print out" tasty baked goods at 24 cpm (cookies per minute). Print-quality settings let you use up to 60 cpi (chips per inch). Plus, a strategically placed bag of ice allows printer to be used for its original purpose (remember to clean between uses, though). 200W AC; UL unlisted. 34 lbs., 12 oz.

971-201A	Cookie Laser Printer	39.99
971-201B	Toner Cartridge	19.99
971-201C	Chocolate Chip Cartridge	4.99

Cheese-ahol

What it lacks in quality it makes up for in savings. This 34-octane fuel has 101 uses—just don't put it in your automobile. Manufactured from government surplus cheese by involuntary Workfare participants in an unnamed dairy state. It's your patriotic duty to buy this stinky fuel, gosh darn it! 5 gal.

971-208   2.50

HAVE A NICE 1979!

JANUARY

					1	2
3	4	5	6	7	8	9
10	11	12	13	14	15	16
17	18	19	20	21	22	23
24	25	26	27	28	29	30
31						

SAVE 90%

1979 Calendars

The Bad Idea Catalog buyers scooped these up for next to nothing in the summer of 1980. Now we're passing the savings on to you. Simply white out the references to Jimmy Carter and pencil in Martin Luther King Jr.'s birthday and you've got a working 2004 calendar. Also good for 2022 and 2042. Several groovy styles from which to choose. Specify Ziggy, Quotable Howard Cosell, Tony Orlando & Dawn, *Mannix*, Bay City Rollers, *Jaws* (pocket size), *Hee Haw, Police Woman,* Have a Nice Day, or *Starsky & Hutch*.

971-223 **Was ~~9.99~~ Now .99**

1939 Calendars

Just $2 each. Some water damage. Specify Charles Lindbergh, Ignatz/ Krazy Kat, WPA Project Pictorial, Ritz Brothers, or Eleanor Roosevelt at the Beach

971-223 **2.00**

Caveat Emptor

This helpful symbol comes to us from the Latin: "Let the buyer beware." Think long and hard before ordering one of the many fine products stamped with this symbol.

Ask yourself the following questions: Will it bite? Is it contagious? Is it a carcinogen? Will it elicit violent behavior from any person, beast, or government agency? Will it burn me? Could I lose a digit or appendage? Could it break my neck or poke out an eye? Will it itch? Will I suffocate? Will the ticking be intolerable? Will it produce or encourage a relapse of asthma or mental illness? Will it permanently stain clothes, carpet, or pets? Will it fit? Will it make a good gift or just a funny one? Will the dog eat it? Will it eat the dog? Will it clash with the drapes? Can I fit in a size 8 or am I just kidding myself? Just how heavy is 1,800 pounds? What will the wife say? If it's so safe, why are they selling it for $1.98? Is it illegal to possess this item within city limits? Is it tax-deductible? How will it affect my property value? Can I handle that amount of amperage? What does it eat? Is the cure worse than the disease? If I get it down, will it stay down? Am I just trying to prove something to my mother? Will it really make me look like Michelle Pfeiffer? Will it make me like Michelle Pfeiffer? If it hurts, will I like it? If pro basketball is legit, how come there are no shutouts? Why is a dime smaller than a nickel? Who is that strange guy at the grocery store? If there is no God, shouldn't there be a lot more seven-legged ants?

If, after asking yourself these questions, you are still foolish enough to make the purchase, we wash our hands of you (after cashing your check, of course).

Office Boy

Many people are disappointed upon learning that there is not, nor ever was, a real Office Boy.

No, this frugal supplier of New Job Smell and other potentially useful corporate products was founded by Albert Finsters, a curmudgeonly old coot now a virtual hermit in the wilds of Milwaukee.

In 1979, Finsters, then a supply clerk for a major midwestern conglomerate, hit upon the idea of ordering extra supplies—then selling them off at a 100 percent profit. On the shoulders of this ingenious strategy Office Boy rose from its humble beginnings, only to plummet back to them when Finsters was forced to retire from the major conglomerate in 1989. That's when we hooked up with him.

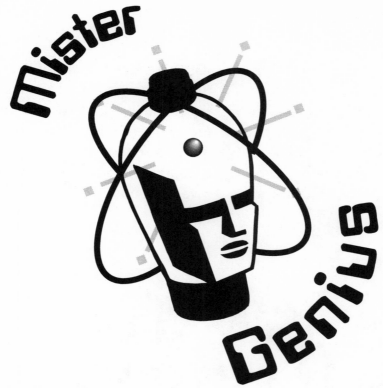

Mister Genius™

Born of humble circumstances in Beverly Hills, California, George Alan Geopoulus was the only son of a working-class Hollywood starlet and her hardworking husband, a wealthy studio executive.

Even at a young age, George showed an aptitude for inventing things, although for the first fifteen years of his life it was limited to excuses for not having brushed his teeth.

During his junior year of high school, George showed great interest in chemistry. So deep was his affection for the subject that he took to sleeping with a pet Bunsen burner (which he called "Sparky").

Never one to waste a college education on himself, George struck out on his own after graduating from high school. He had his name legally changed to George Genius and spent the remainder of his life developing inventions whose simplicity and usefulness have yet to be determined.

Late in his life, George was given an honorary degree in inventionology by Chicago River Community College; hence the moniker "Mister Genius." Alas, Mister Genius is no longer with us. To paraphrase Don McLean's "Starry Night," "This world was never meant for one as cavalier in his handling of explosive compounds as you."

Overseas Import Liquidators

Some of our products are items that just wouldn't sell for someone else. We pick them up for a song, repackage them as a totally different product, put them in the catalog, and see if they get any nibbles. Most of these items come from Overseas Import Liquidators (OIL), a secretive cartel that scours the Seven Seas for big mistakes. Products from such mistakes could include teddy bears with needle-sharp teeth to famous-maker sneakers picked up for a song from a closed-down Malaysian sweatshop.

Freezer Bern

From the frozen tundra of southeastern Tennessee comes Freezer Bern, the oldest name in frozen foods.

Founded during the Civil War by Colonel Beauregard Bernside, the famous Coward of Chattanooga, Freezer Bern first came to prominence when it was identified as the cause of the ptomaine epidemic of 1872, in which thousands succumbed to spoiled canned peaches.

Ruined and penniless, Bernside took a job in North Dakota as a cinder dick for the Pierre Circus Trolley. That winter, upon realizing just how long a walleye carcass will last in subzero weather, he changed the focus of his business from canned to frozen food.

The fact that the enterprise had the word *freezer* in the title made it that much more serendipitous. And the rest, as they say, is obscure history.

"the oldest name in frozen foods"

FREEZER BERN

Mal Sportif

Founded in 1996, Mal Sportif, Inc., believes there is more to sports than sportsmanship.

Hence, its products are geared toward bending, breaking, or circumventing the so-called rules of any given athletic endeavor.

Products that denigrate a sport in favor of comfort or hedonistic pleasure (e.g., the Football-o-Salami) are also up its alley.

Legal Notice

(please read)

The Bad Idea Catalog, Bad Idea Catalog Inc., Bad Idea Worldwide, as well as its/their employees, contractor(s), supplier(s), manufacturer(s), senior management, stockholder(s), trustee(s), board member(s), agent(s), representative(s), affiliate(s), friend(s), relative(s), progeny, indentured servant(s), legal and financial adviser(s), health provider(s), elected official(s), newspaper delivery agent(s), grievance counselor(s), teacher(s), pet(s), teacher's pet(s), spouse(s), social companion(s), POSLQ(s), waiter(s), busboy(s), valet(s) and/or restroom attendant(s), orthodontist(s), massage therapist(s), travel agent(s), neighbor(s), Sherpa guide(s), enemy(ies) (foreign or domestic), favorite musician(s), personal shopper(s), printer(s), book binder(s), temporary employee(s), personal deity(ies) (real or imagined), multiple personalities, biographer(s), manservant(s), girl(s) Friday, barber(s), coiffure(s), hair stylist(s), publicist(s), advertising and/or marketing agency(ies), realtor(s), clothier(s) and subcontractor(s), certified union electrician(s) (Locals 747, 707, 727, 737, DC-10, B-52, 280Z, 90210, 1776, 1492, 1006, 2001, and 007), long-distance provider(s), on-line service(s), Web page creator(s) and/or Internet access provider(s), cable company(ies) and/or illegal cable provider(s), imaginary friend(s), possessing spirit(s), vocal and/or theatrical coach(es), boccie ball teammate(s) or competitor(s), caterer(s), landscaper(s), bail bondsman(men), copy machine repairperson(s), speech/gag and/or ghost writer(s), guardian angel(s), good or evil jinn(s), past, future, or parallel dimensionary life(ves), manicurist(s), creditor(s), beneficiary(ies), haberdasher(s), maître d'(s), bookie(s), mistress(es) (or "sugar daddies"), landlord(s), tenant(s), local public transportation authority, or taxing body hereby disavow any responsibility for, or (to the extent that it is legally expedient) knowledge of, any potential hazards, dangers, disadvantages, dismemberments, disassociations, distempers, discontinuances, disenfranchisements, disqualifications, or disorientations, real or imagined, actual or potential, past, present, or future, foreign or domestic, local or cross-country, national or international, fast or slow, near or far, good, bad, or indifferent, relating to any and all products or services sold in, purchased from, ordered from, received from, manufactured by, distributed by, borrowed from, or inadvertently delivered from *The Bad Idea Catalog* (and that's just the first sentence!). *The Bad Idea Catalog*, its editors, employees, writers, and buyers further swear on their respective mothers' graves that they have no memory of producing, printing, distributing, or even working at the company at the time this particular issue of the catalog was produced. All warranties, implied or expressed, for the products sold herein, whether for the original or current function of the product(s) are null, void, useless, impotent, and as limp as Tiny Tim in that part of *A Christmas Carol* when the Ghost of Christmas Future takes Scrooge to the Cratchit home and they find the little tyke's crutch leaning against his little stool by the fireplace. Seeking civil or criminal action against *The Bad Idea Catalog* for any bad ju-ju arising from use, misuse, or unfortunate proximity to a Bad Idea Catalog product is, in the opinion of our inordinately large legal department, "simply not worth the court filing fee." The legal department further notes that any judgments against *The Bad Idea Catalog* are bound to be appealed, stretching out the case for several years and taking up valuable court time that could be better used for nuisance suits against fast-food franchises whose coffee is just too damn hot. *The Bad Idea Catalog* further notes (against the advice of the legal department) that just because you get a judgment against us doesn't mean you'll ever be able to collect a dime; we have very clever accountants. Nevertheless, we are compelled to give written notice that any expressed warranties must be honored in the following states and territories: AL, AK, AZ, AR, CA, CO, CT, DE, DC, FL, GA, HI, ID, IL, IN, IA, KS, KY, LA, ME, MD, MA, MI, MN, MS, MO, MT, NE, NV, NH, NJ, NM, NY, NC, ND, OH, OK, OR, PA, RI, SC, SD, TN, TX, UT, VT, VA, WA, WV, WI, WY, Guam, Marshall Islands, Northern Mariana Islands, Puerto Rico, and the U.S. Virgin Islands. Any implied warranties must be honored in AL. Residents of AL, AK, AZ, AR, CA, CO, CT, DE, DC, FL, GA, HI, ID, IL, IN, IA, KS, KY, LA, ME, MD, MA, MI, MN, MS, MO, MT, NE, NV, NH, NJ, NM, NY, NC, ND, OH, OK, OR, PA, RI, SC, SD, TN, TX, UT, VT, VA, WA, WV, WI, WY, Guam, Marshall Islands, Northern Mariana Islands, Puerto Rico, and the U.S. Virgin Islands are eligible for a free copy of the voided warranty of any Bad Idea Catalog product; said copy will be painstakingly prepared upon request by the nearsighted monks of the Benedictine Friary of Delph, Luxembourg (ask for "Father Bill"). Residents of AL, AK, AZ, AR, CA, CO, CT, DE, DC, FL, GA, HI, ID, IL, IN, IA, KS, KY, LA, ME, MD, MA, MI, MN, MS, MO, MT, NE, NV, NH, NJ, NM, NY, NC, ND, OH, OK, OR, PA, RI, SC, SD, TN, TX, UT, VT, VA, WA, WV, WI, WY, Guam, Marshall Islands, Northern Mariana Islands, Puerto Rico, and the U.S. Virgin Islands may by law request that this legal notice be read to them in pig Latin; to receive this service, contact comedian Howie Mandel. Any paper cuts, suffocations, or poisonings resulting from misuse of the catalog itself are subject to civil and/or criminal action in CA; conversely, illegal immigrants in CA have no legal recourse whatsoever and, in fact, are subject to arrest and deportation if they even try to contact any government agency. Finally, knowingly ordering a dangerous item from *The Bad Idea Catalog* is expressly and wisely prohibited in all 48 or so states, all U.S. territories and possessions (including Iraq), and all foreign countries except for Canada, where anything goes.

ABOUT THE AUTHORS

Chris Bittler and Dave Markov have been writing together since the early 1980s, when they met on the stage of the famous Night Light Players comedy troupe in Chicago.

Their work includes sketches for the famous *Bozo Show* on WGN-TV, radio spots for the famous *Spiegel Catalog,* and several infamous film, television, and stage projects.

The two make their homes in Chicago and Los Angeles, irrespectively. They are board certified and fully bonded.

courtesy Max St. DuPrix (see page 65)

Chris Bittler

(ditto)

Dave Markov

They're **REAL**.

They're **BAD**.

They're **REAL BAD PRODUCTS**

you can actually buy at:

badideacatalog.com

That's right. Get on your computer and type in http://www.badideacatalog.com and you can be the first on your cyber-block to say, "I paid too much for Bad Idea Catalog merchandise" like:

• **T-shirts!**

• **Coffee mugs!**

• **Other junk!**

PLUS:

• Check out upcoming Bad Idea Catalogs
• Suggest your own Bad Idea products and maybe win something
• Get the scoop on other ridiculous Bad Idea Books
• Send us rude e-mail

And it's all ABSOLUTELY FREE!

(except for the T-shirts and coffee mugs, of course)